THE EXCAVATION OF ARMAGEDDON

THE EXCAVATION OF ARMAGEDDON

By
CLARENCE S. FISHER

Wipf & Stock
PUBLISHERS
Eugene, Oregon

Wipf and Stock Publishers
199 W 8th Ave, Suite 3
Eugene, OR 97401

The Excavation of Armageddon
By Fisher, Clarence S.
ISBN 13: 978-1-55635-451-9
ISBN 10: 1-55635-451-7
Publication date 5/1/2007
Previously published by University of Chicago Press, 1929

FOREWORD

Since Allenby's well-known victories in Palestine during the World War, and also as a result of a famous public utterance of ex-President Roosevelt, the name Armageddon has become a household word even in the Western World of America, which is so far removed from the ancient history of the Near East. To students of the Old Testament the name has always been familiar in its older Hebrew form, Megiddo. No one who has ever read Thutmose III's own records[1] of his great victory against the Asiatics at Armageddon can have failed to be moved by the contagious valor of the young king or the description of the sumptuous spoil which fell into the hands of the Egyptians with the capture of the city.

I shall never forget with what interest and enthusiasm during university days we younger students read this description of the ancient splendor of Megiddo. Ever since those student days, it had always been a dream of mine to excavate this city. In later years the reasons for its power and splendor became more evident and added a more substantial basis to the romantic desire of student dreams. As I look back upon them now, I realize that such youthful visions were to no small extent the outgrowth of boyhood study of the Old Testament with its picturesque references to Megiddo.

It has long been obvious to all historians that Palestine is a middle ground, a kind of ancient "No-Man's Land," lying between the great military powers encamped on either side of it—in Africa the great civilization of the Egyptian Pharaohs; in Asia the kings of Babylonia, the mighty armies of the Assyrian military empire, or the Macedonian rulers of the East. The armies of these great powers, whether marching from Asia into Africa or the reverse, passed up and down the valleys of Palestine and Syria, which lie for the most part between north-and-south ranges and furnish therefore a series of valley highways connecting the two continents.

The bold headland of Mount Carmel, however, its western prom-

---

[1] See the editor's *Ancient Records of Egypt*, Vol. II, §§ 418–35.

ontory projecting into the sea and terminating a ridge which extends
southeastward toward the Jordan Valley, cuts transversely across the
north-and-south ridges of Syria-Palestine. This ridge was the natural
strategic barrier which any enemy in the south would endeavor to
hold against Asiatic invasion from the north (see map, Fig. 3). Simi-
larly, it was inevitably the main line of defense of an Asiatic army
endeavoring to halt an Egyptian invasion coming into southern Palestine. This latter situation is very conclusively illustrated by the history of events in the World War, when the Turkish forces held the
ridge of Carmel against the northward advance of General Allenby's
army.

In its earlier stages, this modern campaign is an extraordinary
repetition of ancient military operations; for Lord Allenby threw his
cavalry through the pass of Megiddo in A.D. 1918, just as the young
Pharaoh Thutmose III made his deadly thrust against the allied
Asiatics by unexpectedly leading a force through this same pass of
Megiddo in the early fifteenth century B.C.

The famous plain to which this pass gave access from the south,
taking its name from Megiddo (Armageddon) or from Esdraelon
(Jezreel), thus became a battlefield where the great powers of neigh-
boring Africa and Asia met in one long struggle after another for
thousands of years, to dispute the political supremacy of the Near
East. It was inevitable that there should grow up here a stronghold
which would command the pass and the plain. The situation of
Megiddo is exactly what we should expect, crowning a prominence on
the northern slopes of the Carmel ridge where it commands an impressive panorama of the plain (Fig. 5) to which the city gave its
name, while at the same time it looks up the pass coming from the
south, which it completely controls (Fig. 4).

In view of the importance of the place and the certainty that the
great conquerors of the past must have left important memorials of
their victories on the plain of Armageddon, it is remarkable that it
has so long awaited investigation. In 1903–5 G. Schumacher, a resi-
dent of Haifa, was commissioned by the Deutsche Orient-Gesellschaft to undertake the excavation of the city. The clearance of so
vast a site (the summit of the mound contains more than 60,000 square
meters, while the slopes would add nearly 150,000 square meters more)

was of course a formidable enterprise. The German expedition confined itself, therefore, chiefly to the excavation of a broad trench in a generally north and south direction through the eastern half of the summit of the mound. Hence Schumacher's excavation penetrated but a limited portion of the mound. It will be found dotted in on the plan (Fig. 11). It is difficult to determine the stratification of an ancient mound from the indications furnished by such a trench; but the volume produced by Schumacher and his colleagues is a useful preliminary suggestion of the nature of the place, although it is unavoidably misleading at many points. That there was insufficient control of the native labor is evidenced by the fact that our workmen picked out the important inscribed fragment of a great stela of Pharaoh Shishak (see Fig. 7) from Schumacher's dump.

Returning from an expedition through Iraq in the turbulent days at the close of the World War, I was able to survey the position of the mound from the hills of Nazareth on the north, but the marshy plain below made it impossible to cross and examine the mound at close range. Owing to the shortness of the time at our disposal, we were unable to make the long detour around the plain. Two years later, however, I went over the mound with Professor Garstang, the Director of Antiquities of the Palestine government, and his assistant, Mr. Phythian Adams. This visit increased my interest in the place, and I was greatly impressed with the importance of a thorough investigation and systematic clearance of the mound.

In May, 1925, Mr. John D. Rockefeller, Jr., generously indicated his willingness to finance the proposed excavation of Armageddon for a period of five years to begin July 1, 1925. The expedition was therefore organized in the summer of that year under Dr. Clarence S. Fisher as field director. In telling the story of the initial stages of the expedition and the erection of the headquarters house, Dr. Fisher has shown commendable reserve regarding the complications involved. The marshes immediately on the north of the expedition headquarters have been the source of very serious and disheartening difficulties. The malarial mosquito infests the region, and long before the house was ready for occupancy all the members of the expedition were prostrated by this devastating scourge. Furthermore, since the actual process of excavation began, the members of the staff have been

repeatedly laid low; and on one occasion when His Excellency the
High Commissioner, Lord Plumer, was kind enough to visit the work
of the expedition, every member of the staff was in bed with malaria
and there was no one to receive him. The drainage of these neighbor-
ing swamps and marshes is not easy, for several reasons, not least the
wandering herds of the natives. Hoofs, sinking deep into the mud,
disturb buried tile drains so that the spring freshets tear up and completely destroy all such drainage works. It is a pleasure to record
here the very helpful co-operation of the Public Health Service of the
Palestine government. As a result of this assistance it has been possible to organize against the malarial pest. We now have a native patrol
which constantly visits and controls all the drainage channels and,
when any undrained pool is found, arranges for its immediate drainage. Such measures as this, combined with the use of dilute paris
green (not sufficiently strong to poison the native cattle) scattered
on the surface of the water, have greatly improved health conditions
at Megiddo; while a well-screened house and beds equipped with
moustiquaires have very essentially mitigated the danger from
malaria.

With the cessation of the rains in the spring of 1926, it was possible
to begin work; and a very creditable amount of clearance was accom-
plished in that season, in spite of the delays and difficulties inevitably
following upon the ravages of malaria.

As Dr. Fisher has clearly indicated, the operations at Megiddo
fell into two parts: first, the clearance of the eastern slopes in order
to salvage all ancient evidence in this region and thus to prepare an
area of investigated territory in which the large accumulation of
débris from the excavations on the summit of the mound might be
dumped; second, the excavation of the summit of the mound itself.
It was planned from the beginning that merely exploratory trenches
such as those excavated by the earlier expedition would not be em-
ployed at Megiddo. The excavations on the slope to prepare space
for the dump would not, of course, disclose stratigraphic deposits of
the ancient débris. But on the summit itself, the plan of campaign was
to organize a series of clearances each one of which should strip off
an entire ancient stratum over a considerable area. An ideal arrangement would have provided for stripping off the uppermost stratum

over the entire surface of the mound, but many practical considerations made this ideal plan entirely unfeasible. An area in the eastern half of the mound which gave promise of containing the important buildings was therefore laid out as the limit of the excavation, and the removal of each stratum was to be limited by the boundary of this area. The materials from Stratum I and Stratum II were surveyed as expeditiously as possible and then cleared away. The work then penetrated into Stratum III.

Early in the work of the expedition a significant indication of the important monuments which this mound must once have covered unexpectedly appeared. On my first arrival at the mound after work had begun in the spring of 1926, Dr. Fisher informed me that a fragment inscribed with Egyptian hieroglyphs had been brought down from the top of the mound as a building block during the construction of the house. It was with considerable satisfaction on the first sunny day after the rains had diminished that I was able to make out the name of Shishak or Sheshonk I, in hieroglyphs very dimly glimmering from a badly weather-worn and almost illegible inscribed stone surface. As a lad in a country Sunday school, I had so often read the familiar words of the Old Testament historian in I Kings 14:25–26, that they came back to me very vividly as this record of the ancient conqueror's name, found in the midst of ruins of one of his captured cities, became slowly legible.

And it came to pass in the fifth year of king Rehoboam, that Shishak king of Egypt came up against Jerusalem: and he took away the treasures of the house of the Lord, and the treasures of the king's house; he even took away all: and he took away all the shields of gold which Solomon had made.

The fragment preserved was part of the top of a large round-topped stela, and the round top could be restored on the basis of the portion preserved, so as to show that the great slab was about 5 feet wide. Judging from the proportions of similar monuments, such as the famous "Israel Stela," Shishak's monument at Megiddo will therefore have been some 10 feet high (Fig. 9). As the preserved fragment is about 20 inches thick, the monument must have been a massive and impressive memorial. A comparison with other similar monuments which have survived in Egypt (Fig. 8) shows that it contained above and extending up into the top a relief scene depicting the king worshiping the god Amon, while an inscription recording the king's victories engraved in horizontal lines extending entirely across the stela will have occupied the lower portion. This great historical record at Megiddo, commemorating the campaign of Shishak in Palestine as recorded in the Old Testament, may even have contained the name of Jerusalem written in Egyptian hieroglyphs, although a hieroglyphic writing of the name Jerusalem has never yet been found. Shishak's list on the walls of the temple at Karnak in Egypt does not mention it.

After the erection of this monument in the tenth century B.C., the complete collapse of Egyptian power left Shishak's huge stela a prey to the Pharaoh's enemies, and it was apparently broken up into building-stones. One of these blocks, and luckily the one containing the Pharaoh's name, after having lain doubtless for many centuries incorporated in the masonry of a stone wall, was thrown out by Schumacher's workmen and lay for twenty years on the summit of the mound of Megiddo, until it was brought down to our house by the Palestinian workmen and one of our Egyptian foremen accidentally noticed the hieroglyphs which it bore. It is very much to be hoped that the buildings which we have still to excavate at Megiddo may disclose additional fragments of this important monument, so that we can reconstruct and restore it. But whether or not this good fortune befalls the work of the expedition, the discovery of this fragment is a demonstration of the important character of the historical records which were once erected at Megiddo and in all probability still lie buried in the mound.

With the advance of the spring of 1927 the health of the expedition, including that of Dr. Fisher himself, was in a very precarious state. He was therefore appointed as advisory director, with the immediate task of completing a very much needed chronologically arranged catalogue or corpus of the pottery of Palestine. This is a kind of reference book which is entirely lacking throughout the range of Oriental archaeology; and the production of such an indispensable work of reference will be of the greatest assistance to all future research in Palestine, for it will enable us in coming excavations much more easily to date the successive strata by means of the potsherds, which serve as the archaeologist's fossils. This work is now approaching completion and will appear in the series of our researches known as "Oriental Institute Publications."

Dr. Fisher's successor in immediate charge of the work on the mound of Megiddo is Mr. P. L. O. Guy, formerly assistant director, and for a time acting director, of the Department of Antiquities in the Palestine government. He is at present continuing the excavations. At this writing the clearance of Stratum III has for the first time disclosed a town plan, with the buildings and streets, including large stables which, as Mr. Guy noted, can hardly be anything else than the stables of Solomon (I Kings 9:15–19; 10:10). A preliminary report on these further excavations will soon follow this present bulletin. Through expropriation by the Palestine government the Oriental Institute is soon to acquire rights including the whole site, and the excavations are to be extended over the entire mound during the spring and summer of 1929.

JAMES HENRY BREASTED

THE ORIENTAL INSTITUTE
UNIVERSITY OF CHICAGO
December 20, 1928

TABLE OF CONTENTS

I

TOPOGRAPHY AND HISTORY

For most of us the name Armageddon has become simply a household term designating some vital combat or a great final struggle for supremacy. We forget that it was once the name of a very real place, one that in the contests for world-power which constantly pitted the empires of the ancient world against one another, played a conspicuous part and earned for itself the reputation which it now bears. The "Field of Armageddon," or, as we know it at present, the Valley of Esdraelon, was the name given to the depression across the northern end of Palestine, beginning at the sea, on the landward slopes of Mount Carmel, and extending toward the southeast as far as the village of Jezreel, which gives its name to a narrower extension of the valley. Finally it opens out into the valley of the Jordan opposite Beth Shean. It was the natural and easy road between the sea coast and the rich countries beyond the river.

To understand fully its value in the drama of history, one must ride up from Haifa on a clear spring morning. As the road ascends to Nazareth, winding up the sides of the hills which form the northern rampart of the plain, it now and again skirts the edge of these hills and affords brief glimpses of the plain spread out far below, its undulations flattened by the distance. The varying sizes and shapes of the fields, long narrow strips and squares, with their different crops, give the impression of a splendid rug with a checkered pattern in delicate tones of green and brown. But it is when the road leaves Nazareth, and on its way toward Samaria and Jerusalem begins its quick and tortuous descent, that the plain expands stretched out far below in its whole beauty and extent.

Peaceful as may be the picture that now presents itself (cf. Fig. 5), there were times in history when it formed the setting for spectacles of quite another character. Just because it was, as it still is, the most fertile and well-watered plain of Palestine, situated midway on the great highway connecting Egypt with Babylonia and the East, it

1

Fig. 2.—Megiddo from the northeast, near the track to Afuleh. The expedition headquarters at the right

offered the best possible camping ground for an army, and a base for
their further military operations in every direction. It yielded abundant crops and also pasturage during most of the year for numerous
flocks and herds.

From the hills above Nazareth, on a clear day when the lights and
shadows are favorable, one can see far over on the opposite (southern)
side of the plain a flat-topped knoll nestling against the hills that form
the frontier between the sea and the higher interior. This is the site of
Armageddon, the "Hill of Megiddo," once the key to the possession of
the entire plain (Figs. 1–2). Today all suggestion of its importance has
vanished. Even its name has been lost in its native appellation of Tell
el-Mutesellim. But under its former name it has left an undying
imprint on the pages of ancient annals. It was never so extensive a
city as Gaza, Hazor, or Samaria, but depended for its importance
upon its strategic position commanding the inner end of one of the
main passes across the range of hills from the coast.

Reference to the map of Palestine (Fig. 3) will show the reasons
for the importance of Megiddo as a fortress. The route from Egypt
into Asia followed first the easy course up the coast through Gaza,
sometimes skirting the sea shore and again swinging inland through
the rich Plain of Sharon. Along the route other roads branched off
into the hilly country of the interior to the east, to towns such as
Lachish, Gezer, and Beth Shemesh, each a center of fertile though
limited territory and the nucleus of some minor kingdom. From
Caesarea northward the road was partly barred by the formidable
transverse rampart of Mount Carmel, which had to be doubled at the
seaward end before the entrance to the Valley of Esdraelon could be
reached. From the coast near Caesarea there were several short routes
across the barrier of the Carmel ridge which obviated this difficulty.
Of these the most important may be called for historical reasons the
Pass of Megiddo (Fig. 4), for it was the most direct, although not the
most easy of passage. Passing the town of Aruna and proceeding
through the Wadi Arah, it emerged on the central plain at Megiddo.
Commanding thus the most direct pass across the transverse ridge of
Carmel, Megiddo was a stronghold of decisive strategic importance.
Once this powerful fortress was gained, there offered many alternative
routes to points north and east. First was the direct route down the

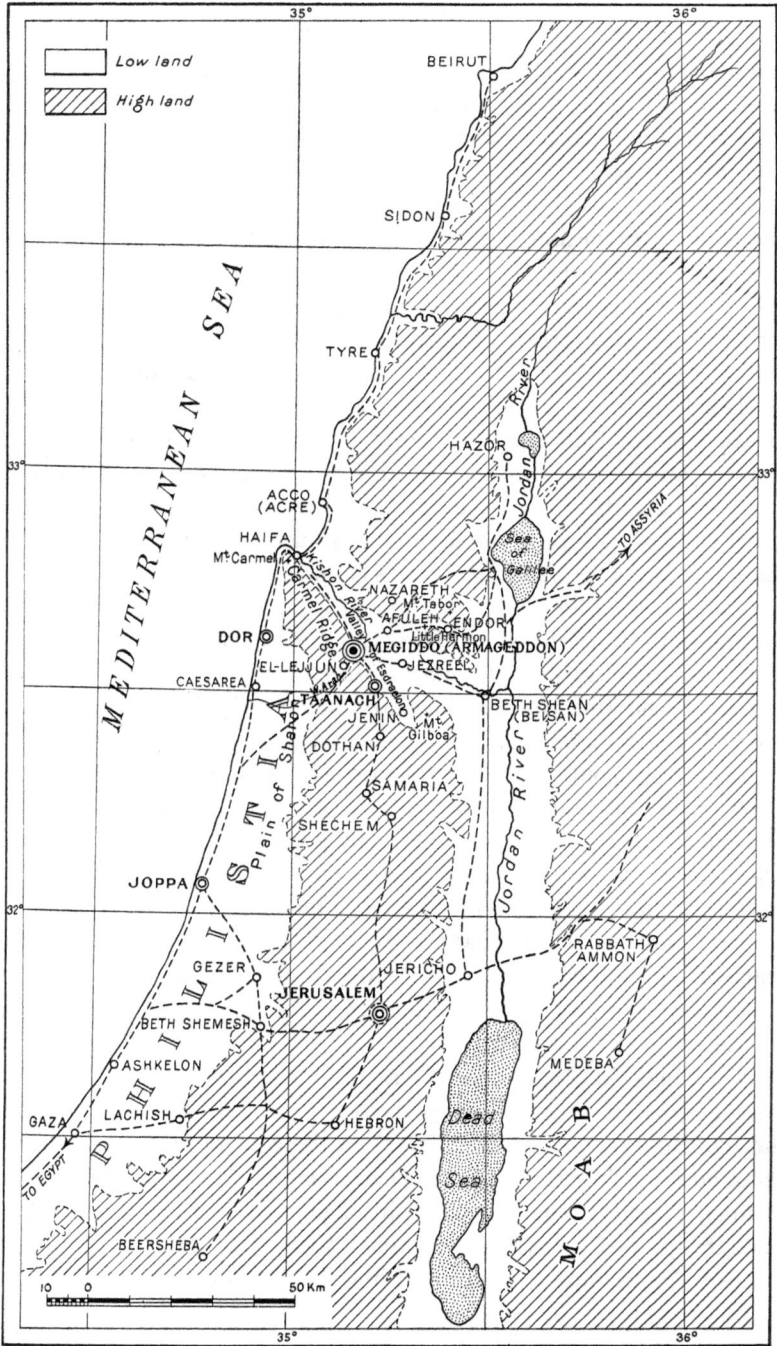

FIG. 3.—Map of Palestine showing the relation of Megiddo to the trade routes

plain past Jezreel and Beth Shean and then northward up the Jordan. A second followed this same course as far as Jezreel and then turned more toward the north, crossing the low eastern talus of Little Hermon and reaching the Jordan Valley north of Beth Shean. A third skirted this hill, passing through Nain and Endor and coming out into the other routes. The great northern route crossed the one steep pass at Nazareth and then divided, one road going toward the

FIG. 4.—A modern caravan in the Pass of Megiddo

Sea of Galilee, the other toward Hazor, that mighty stronghold of the king who oppressed Israel during the time of the Judges.

The modern road from the north to Megiddo passes through Afuleh, eight miles away from the great mound. To reach Megiddo the main road is left here and one travels across a rough field track, quite passable in summer, but, after the winter rains have set in, a snare for the unwary motorist. In order to avoid the course of the river Kishon, the track makes a long detour to the south, passing along the eastern face of the broad mound of Megiddo at a distance of not more than a kilometer. From this point the hill is seen in one of its most impressive aspects (cf. Fig. 2), capping a long gentle rise in the plain and standing out sharp and clear against the range of hills behind it.

But another equally impressive picture is one that the traveler never sees. It is from the slopes of this same background of hills looking toward the east (Fig. 1). The spot is remote from traveled roads and native villages, and only an occasional flock of goats or a transient Bedouin encampment infuses life into the view. The little valley between Megiddo and this vantage point was the route of the former road from the outlet of the pass. Toward the left, that is, on the north side of the mound, was the gate to the ancient city. Once a walled and towered fortress, it has become in outward appearance a worn and weathered heap of débris and scattered stones. Originally the hill was much smaller in extent, being an isolated rock beside a spring, and nearly half the present height represents the accumulations of rubbish resulting from the destruction by fire and siege of many superimposed cities. These were built one after another upon the same site and often with the materials taken from the ruins of the preceding town—a record of human occupation extending from the earliest civilized man down to the Hellenistic age, when its history ceased. Under the Romans a new camp was laid out a kilometer to the south, nearer to the outlet of the pass, leaving the earlier hill to other uses.

Ascending now to the summit of our hill, we command an extensive panorama of the area overlooked by the fortress (Fig. 5). Beginning at the west are the towering masses of Mount Carmel, its sides broken up by deep, shadowy ravines. Unfolding from behind its northern edge and hiding a view of the sea, a range of hills stretches along the northern edge of the plain as far eastward as Nazareth. Here the range is broken by a deep inset, from the midst of which rises the peculiar conical peak of Tabor. Farther east is the long, smooth contour of Little Hermon. Great Hermon itself is hidden from Megiddo by the hills behind Nazareth, but glimpses of it can be obtained along the road from Megiddo southeastward to Taanach and Jenin. Esdraelon, which for most of its western extent rises but little above the level of the Mediterranean, suddenly drops away at its eastern end between Little Hermon and its opposite neighbor, Mount Gilboa, known to all of us as the scene of the tragic defeat of the Hebrew army under Saul. At Beth Shean its level is already over a hundred meters below the sea. The drop is quite apparent, silhouetted against the far distant

Nazareth   Mt. Tabor
↓   ↓

FIG. 5.—Panorama from summit of Megiddo

Little Hermon   Beth Shean   Mt. Gilboa
    ↓   ↓   Jezreel   ↓
                       ↓

over the Valley of Esdraelon or Armageddon

mountains of Moab. Against this same background stands out the Arab village which now covers the site of Jezreel.

Between the slopes of Gilboa and Megiddo, extending some kilometers to the south, is a wide fertile valley, an offshoot from the greater central plain. Since our photograph does not extend far enough to include this, a word of description must suffice. At the southern end of this valley is Jenin, standing in the midst of green gardens at the outlet of a ravine that forms a natural highway to Dothan and its famous plain. From Jenin the hills sweep on toward south and west until they join up with Carmel, thus completing the circuit of the plain. About eight kilometers away in the general direction of Jenin rises the fine mound covering the ruins of Taanach, a sister town to Megiddo and often mentioned with her in the Scriptures. In the near foreground is the little modern village of el-Lejjun, its name a reminder of the Roman legion that once was stationed here. Just to the west of this is the entrance of the Wadi Arah and the Pass of Megiddo. At present a rough road runs through the wadi to Aruna. Its usefulness is due in great part to the Romans, who, by cutting away projecting rock walls and widening and lowering the level of the road, made it much more passable than it ever could have been in the time of the Pharaohs and the Hebrew kings.

In earlier times traversing the Wadi Arah was always a difficult matter, as even foot soldiers could proceed in it only two abreast and never with any great speed. Along its sides were numerous little ravines, each containing a tiny well-hidden village, and at many places the pass was overlooked by steep hills. Thus the wadi could have been easily defended by a few men, had any serious effort been made to do so. It would appear, however, that, while forming a sufficient highway for files of laden animals in caravans, the difficulties for the passage of any large body of troops were recognized and its defense was regarded as unnecessary. Certainly Thutmose III, during his use of it, records no opposition.

The campaign of this Egyptian ruler is one of the most illuminating events in connection with the plain and its guardian fortress, of which we have any record. The episode is so dramatic and the record left of it by Thutmose on the temple walls of Karnak so human in its details that it will always stand out as a fascinating picture of the

military operations of that period, although doubtless many other
equally spectacular crossings must have been made both before and
after his time.

It will be remembered that Thutmose III in the year 1479 B.C.
began a campaign into Palestine and Syria. By May 13 of that year
he had reached Aruna, on the coast side of the Wadi Arah, and had
halted there to consider ways and means of crossing into the Plain of
Armageddon. At a meeting of his staff several routes were proposed.
Thutmose himself was strongly in favor of the direct road to the
Wadi Arah. His officers, because they knew the roughness and difficulty of this route, endeavored to dissuade him from attempting it.
Perhaps Thutmose had received private information that the pass
was left unguarded and that the inhabitants of the small villages along
the route had, at the rumors of his near approach, fled to the shelter of
Taanach and Megiddo. However this may be, the king had his way,
and next morning led his men on the advance through the pass. By
late afternoon they had debouched upon the plain in the neighborhood
of the modern el-Lejjun and made camp along the banks of the stream
flowing from the Ain es-Sitt.

Some time before this, the King of Kadesh had made a coalition
against Egypt with most of the other rulers of the states of Syria and
Palestine, and had gathered at Megiddo a vast host to withstand the
progress of Thutmose. The allies' troops overflowed the town and
their main camp was spread on the top of the low hills just south of
the fortress. Early next morning an advance was made in three columns against the town. One Egyptian corps followed the main road
passing to the west of the town, another followed the eastern road,
while the center stormed the camp. The enemy, it appears, were
completely surprised by the attack, although it is inconceivable that
they had not known of the presence of the Egyptians the evening before and made some preparations for defense. The surprise may be
explained by the presence of one of the heavy mists that cover the
plain at this season of the year, which effectually concealed the Egyptians until they were close upon the enemy. The rout was complete
and the enemy retreated in such disorder that many of their leaders
had to be hauled up over the town walls, the entrance, as we have seen,
having been at the opposite end of the town. The Egyptian troops now

made a mistake, incurring thereby the scorn of their king. Instead of at once following up their victory, they stopped to gather in the loot of the deserted camp. Within the walls was the entire group of kings forming the coalition; and, had they been taken with the town, the political result of Thutmose's ultimate capture of the place would have been greatly increased. As it was, during the night they escaped northward.

In our own time this exploit has been paralleled by General Allenby, whose mounted troops made a quick flanking movement through the pass and forced the surrender of a large body of Turkish troops in the Plain of Esdraelon, before they could make their escape through its numerous outlets. So sudden was this movement that General von Sanders, the commander of the Turkish army, had barely time to escape, clothed in a pair of pajamas, in his motor car.

Not until the mound is completely excavated and virgin rock is reached, can we determine the full number of strata which it contains. The preliminary clearances of Schumacher in 1903–5 uncovered a well-built series of stone buildings at a depth of 12 meters below the summit, and rock was found at least 5 meters farther down. In the first 3 meters of the Oriental Institute excavations we cleared two well-defined town levels and below them reached a third dating to the Israelite period, of the ninth century B.C. Thus we can form some idea of the number of separate stages in the history of Megiddo which we may expect to find.

As already pointed out, Megiddo had many advantages as an ideal place of settlement. The Palestinian from the earliest times has always placed his dwelling upon the highest available hill near his fields. From it he could keep a close watch upon his crops and upon the herds grazing over the tract of land below him; and, when danger was sighted, the flocks and herds, as well as the workers in the fields, could be instantly called within a safe distance. Our hill of Megiddo not only offered a superb vantage ground of great military strength, but also enjoyed that greater boon in this arid country, a constant and plentiful water supply. From the foot of the northern slope issues the Ain el-Kubbi (see map, Fig. 6); to the south is another spring, and three others lie within a few hundred meters of the site. The abundance of

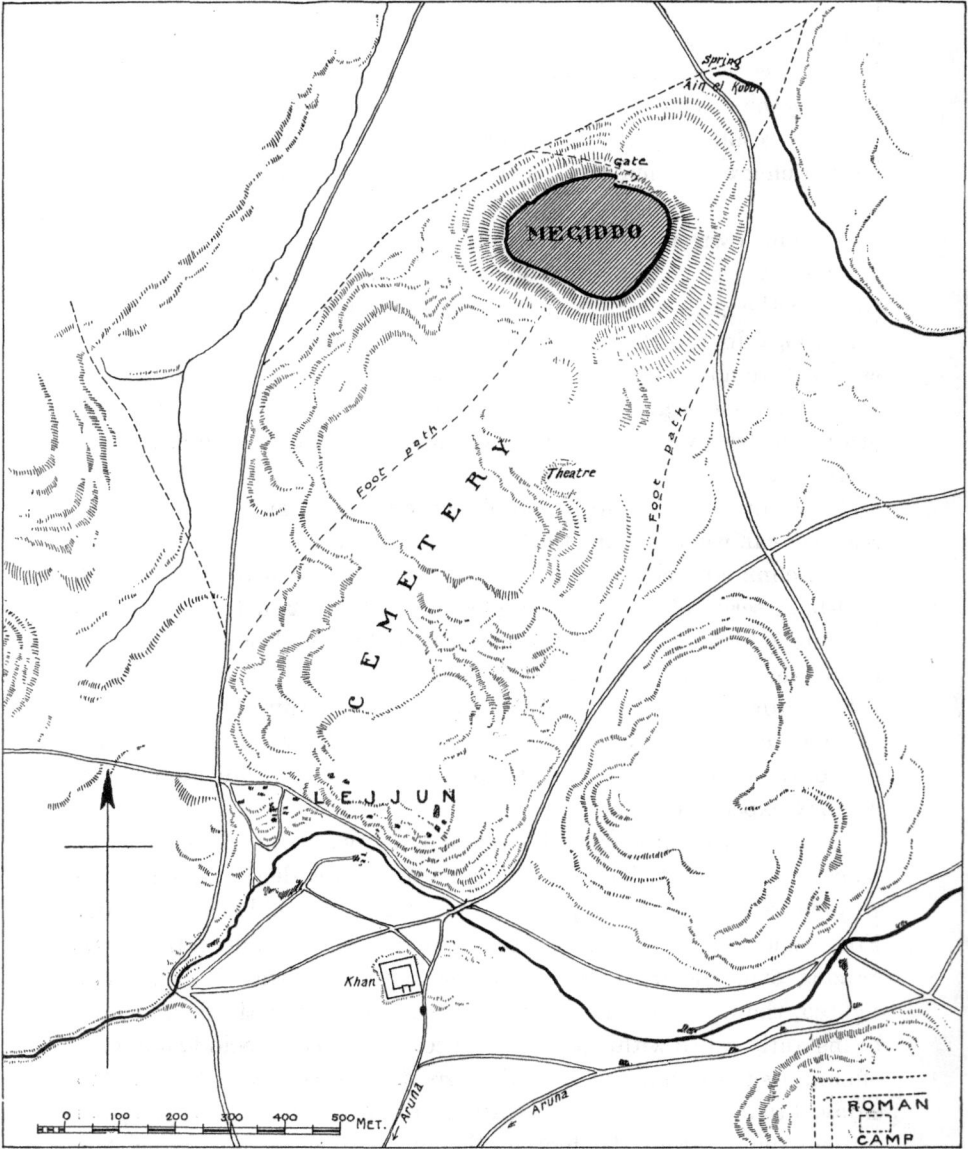

Fig. 6.—Map of the environs of Megiddo (after Schumacher)

these, more than in any other town of Palestine, made them famous as the "Waters of Megiddo."

Whether its earliest inhabitants were indigenous or some band of immigrants seeking a new home remains to be determined. In any event, they found Megiddo well adapted to their purpose. There were any number of natural caverns honeycombing the sides of the hill, and these served as the first dwellings. It would be the rarest of good fortune to find one of these intact with its priceless collection of pottery, implements, and weapons, since every cave would have been used and re-used in succeeding ages as tomb, storage place, or even cistern; but the original contents would have been thrown aside into the rubbish and have remained buried in the accumulating débris of the following ages. We have found early caves on the eastern slope of the hill; from their vicinity and from other parts of the hill there have come specimens of flint and stone implements sufficient, at least, to prove the presence of prehistoric man on the site.

With the entrance of the Semitic stocks into the land, the advancement of civilization was more rapid. Man began to devise more comfortable quarters for himself. Religion developed and shrines were needed for his gods. Growing wealth brought a desire for finer things, especially for woman: jewelry for her person and better utensils for her cooking and her household work. Armor and clothing came more and more into use and new trades and occupations sprang up.

In building, the first material was clay, which was found in every region and was easily moved to the place of construction. At first it was used either *en masse*, like adobe, or in large, roughly shaped blocks. The fashioning of bricks easily handled and bonded into one another to form a stable wall was a matter of acquired skill in manipulating the materials. Roofs in all the early periods were constructed of trunks of trees covered with reed mats and a layer of clay. Thus built, houses of the early period had a brief life and had to be repaired and rebuilt at short intervals. It was, however, the great catastrophes of history that formed the punctuations marking our archaeological periods. A great pestilence would nearly wipe out the inhabitants of a town and send the survivors fleeing to other, healthier districts. The town under sun, wind, and rain rapidly disintegrated and, when later some of the former inhabitants or their offspring returned, they had to rebuild the place entirely. Then again an invading army would leave the town a heap of smoking débris. In both cases the process of rebuilding followed but one method. None of the débris was cleared away. All usable material was salvaged and the remainder simply

FIG. 7A.—Fragment of the Shishak stela. Scale about 1 to 3

leveled off, the new town rising upon the resulting platform. In this manner the hill rose higher and higher, and each increase in height rendered it more impregnable than before. Half the height of the hill at Megiddo is due to the succession of many such destructions and rebuildings.

We have seen how in the time of Thutmose III Megiddo was a strongly fortified post, the chief town of a wealthy kingdom. His record is our first notice of any town here, but the Megiddo of his day

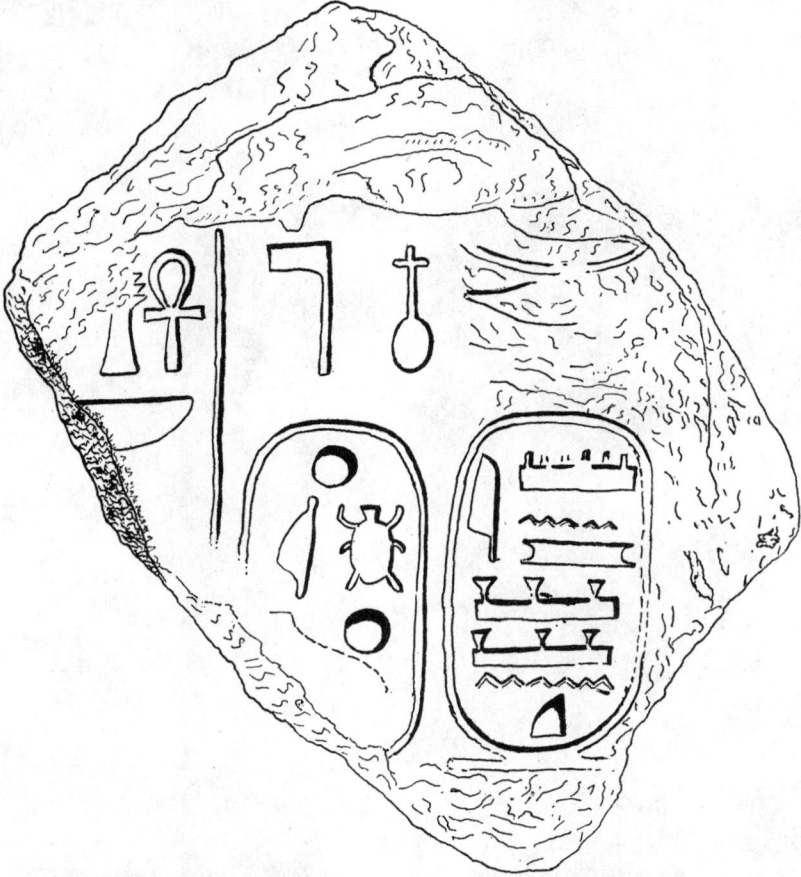

FIG. 7B.—Facsimile drawing of the fragment of the Shishak stela.—Compare Fig. 9. Traces of signs are visible over the second cartouche; they suggest *nb yrt yḫt*, "Lord of Presenting Offerings," a title which is often applied to Sheshonk I. The difficulty with this reading is that the *nb* sign at the top is written differently in the column at the left, where the entire interior of the sign is recessed, whereas in the column at the right it would be merely incised in contour.—EDITOR.

was only the product of many ages of growth and prosperity the length of whose duration remains to be discovered. Having captured the town, it was necessary for Thutmose to preserve it not only as a base of further operations but as part of a chain of posts along his

Fig. 8.—Stela of Amenhotep III, model for restoration of Shishak stela (Fig. 9)

FIG. 9.—Restoration of Shishak stela on basis of Fig. 8. Cf. note, p. 16.

road back to Egypt. He therefore probably restored such parts of the
walls as had been damaged during his siege, and planted a strong garrison in it. When we reach the level corresponding in regular sequence
to his time, we may expect to find a stela commemorating the capture
and the establishment of such a garrison. Many years later both Seti
I and Ramses II erected such stelae at Beth Shean (modern Beisan).

Our next date in the history of Megiddo is about 970 B.C., when
Solomon is said to have fortified and garrisoned the place. On the
south edge of the summit there are remains of a large structure of
unmistakably Israelite character, as proved by similarity in plan and
structure to the palace found at Samaria built by Omri about 875
B.C. This Megiddo building was destroyed during the invasion of
Shishak in 932 B.C. A fragment of his stela (Fig. 7; cf. Figs. 8–9) found
here proved that he occupied the town for a time at least. The buildings
were reconstructed during the reign of Ahab in 870 B.C. Only a small
building of this period has been cleared on the summit. It likewise
was destroyed, and later its ruins were repaired with rough rubble
and used as the foundations of the central building of a sanctuary of
Astarte. The minor halls and rooms grouped around this new and
sacred compound were built of rubble and large sun-dried bricks.
Presently the whole complex was destroyed by fire, the limestone
altars with the incense brazier of the shrine being first thrown down.
Several storerooms were found filled with pottery jars and jugs buried
in the ashes.

At the next stage, we find on the summit a large rectangular fort
with small irregular houses grouped around it. Narrow lanes, with
covered water channels running down their centers, intersected the
town. The date of this stratum is uncertain. The Astarte level belonged between 800 and 600 B.C., while the topmost town, the final
occupation on the hill, was inhabited not later than 350 B.C. To some
extent this topmost town was a continuation of the one beneath, with
the fort plan retained; but the houses were inferior in construction
and arranged without system, like a poor modern Arab village. When
at length this topmost settlement also had fallen into ruin, Megiddo as
a site and even as a name passed out of man's memory. The mound
became the haunt of foxes and other animals, attracted by the presence
of a few isolated graves built into the remaining walls of houses. Such
in brief is our present knowledge of Megiddo.

NOTE ON FIG. 9.—The existing fragment (Fig. 7) is shown in the upper right-
hand portion of the relief scene occupying the top of the Shishak stela as restored. The curve still observable on the outer edge of the fragment, together with
the inscription, especially the two cartouches, makes the position of the fragment
certain. The preserved curve furthermore makes possible a rough calculation
of the original width. The scale is about 1:14.

II

ORGANIZATION

After the preliminary arrangements for the expedition were made with Dr. Breasted in Chicago early in the summer of 1925, preparations for departure were accelerated and, with my nephew as one of the staff, I was able to sail by the quickest route from New York on August 18. All the equipment was to follow on a slower steamer direct to Haifa in the care of Mr. Higgins, the engineer of the expedition, and Mr. DeLoach, his assistant. Being thus able to travel lightly and swiftly across Europe, we arrived in Alexandria on September 1. Proceeding to Cairo, I arranged for our staff of Egyptians, men whom I had previously had with me on different earlier expeditions. They had received careful training in excavating, and were able intelligently to follow out walls and strata. I collected additional equipment also, such as a light railway and recording supplies. Most of the latter I had ordered from America as soon as the expedition was assured. The additional equipment was to be forwarded direct to Haifa, whither the Egyptian workmen were to proceed a few days before we should need them at Megiddo. Then we went up by train to Jerusalem, where matters of official routine in regard to our expedition were quickly arranged with the ever courteous and helpful Professor Garstang, then Director of Antiquities. Soon we were off to Haifa, where several days were lost in waiting for the Egyptians, whom religious holidays and the closing of the passport bureau in Cairo had detained. In the meantime we secured some old army tents for temporary shelter while our permanent camp was being built. When all was ready, the men went on in the morning to Megiddo with the heavier equipment, and we followed in another car with a multitude of smaller parcels, arriving at the hill late in the afternoon.

The men had pitched our tents on a level spot under the northern lee of the hill and near a spring, the Ain el-Kubbi—a beautiful spot with an innocent look, but soon to undeceive us! One large tent we used for sleeping as well as for a dining-room and office, while another

17

was for the workmen. A small, round tent was the cook's domain. It was too late to make a tour of the hill that day, but next morning we were up early and inspected the entire mound. It was the second time I had seen the place, as I had paid it a short visit several years before when on the way to Jerusalem from Beisan. Many of the trenches made in 1903–5 by Dr. Schumacher under the auspices of the Deutsche Orient-Gesellschaft were still visible, although partly filled up with loose stones and fallen earth. The people of el-Lejjun had been busy since my first visit, quarrying into the old masonry exposed by the former excavations, and many a shining new house in the village had an Israelite origin.

During the afternoon an old gentleman, accompanied by a bright-looking young man, rode up and asked for an interview. He was Hassan Effendi, a local magnate, with whom we were to become better acquainted later on. He had heard that we had come to excavate the hill and wished to spy out the situation. Unfortunately Tell el-Mutesellim is in the hands of private owners living in Umm el-Fahm, and we had to negotiate either its lease or its purchase with these people. As it turned out, there were some ninety separate owners holding varying amounts of shares. As the largest individual holder, Hassan was eager to serve as agent for all the rest.

This land question was one of our early trials and to get fair treatment we ultimately had to have recourse to a government commission. The regular assessor of lands and crops came over, measured up the area which we had staked out for our first three years' work, and then fixed the sum which we would have to pay as rental per year. We paid in advance for three years, and to Hassan's chagrin we insisted on ourselves distributing to each owner his particular share of the rent. Although Hassan saw that we had got the better of him, he must have perceived our good intentions, for he later became quite a good friend, paying many visits and consuming large quantities of our coffee and cigarettes. Had we paid the rental money through him, his business acumen would undoubtedly have led him to leave a large percentage of it in his own pockets as commission. For his reputation of being the richest man in the district is well grounded. I am sure that by looking after their interests in this way we gained a strong hold on the feelings of the villagers from whose ranks we needed later to draft our

workpeople. It also made us quite independent in employing and dis-
missing our local workmen and workwomen.

A few days after our arrival we moved the tents to the edge of a
plateau which extends out from the northern side of the main hill,
just above the spring. Charming as the lower camping ground might
be, we found that it had too many mosquitoes and was too near the
track of numerous flocks of goats and sheep to be pleasant. Soon after
we were settled in the new quarters, the rest of our party arrived and
we erected a third large tent to be used solely as an office and dining-
room. I had also brought from Jerusalem a single green canvas tent
with full equipment, and this was turned over to Mr. Higgins for his
office and living quarters. We were now able to arrange the permanent organization. To Mr. Higgins was given the task of beginning
the preliminary survey of the *tell*, and also the oversight of the construction of the headquarters. The land question was then not quite
settled, but I had already instructed the Egyptians to clear out some
of the old trenches in order to provide permanent ways for the light
railway. I had them also make a clearance along the south edge of the
summit to determine whether the Israelite buildings found there continued toward the west.

After some consideration the eastern end of the plateau on which
our camp was pitched was chosen as the site for the house. This was
against the desire of Hassan and some of the other owners, but our
lease left the matter in our hands. We had sounded the plain below as
a possible alternative in case we were prevented from using the terrace, but found the earth there too deep to give us stable foundations.
It would furthermore have been open to the same objections that
obtained near the spring. The terrace location was the most practicable, as we were above, though still near, our water supply and were
just below the side of the hill where, for the first few years at least, our
work was to be concentrated. The house stands over part of the ancient site, but only on strata of the latest period. It is the plan to
leave this portion until the close of the work, then remove the house,
examine and record the area, and finally turn it back to the owners in
cultivable condition.

As we purposed making a long stay at Megiddo, permanent camp
life under the usual conditions, especially during the heavy rains of

winter, could not be thought of. For hard work continuing through
six months each year over a long period of years, one had to have
good sleeping quarters and be adequately protected from the weather
and the malarial mosquitoes. There must be a safe place for the study
and storage of antiquities and field records, and also proper rooms for
making and storing the large number of photographic plates we should
require to complete our record of the work, besides drafting-room,
workrooms, shops, and offices. A house was therefore planned which
would give us all these conveniences. A road was laid out leading up
the slope from the main road at the spring to the new site, and stones
were collected from all over the site for the building. Only stones
which were either loose in the débris or in the upper courses of walls
already excavated were taken and in the latter case the lower courses
were left to be checked up on the plans later on. Mr. Higgins engaged
a head contractor from Sidon, who brought with him several trained
masons from Syria, and work was begun. Fortunately the winter
rains set in later that year than usual, for it was a race against time.
The wings and smaller outbuildings were hurried, so that when our
first great storm came on, late in November, we had some rooms ready
for occupancy. This storm flattened out our tents, but luckily did no
real damage. Early in December we had the roof over the main building in place and covered with its layer of composition roofing, and we
were then able to proceed at a more leisurely gait with the interior.

The rectangular compound (Fig. 10) consists of walls and buildings inclosing two courts, the outer court separated from the inner by
a special building for the non-European staff. The main gate is on
the north side (far side in Fig. 10, at right) at the top of the road, and
another gate at the rear is the work entrance. The main gate opens into the outer court, at the inner end of which is a carpenter shop and an
open garage for three or four cars. I may say here that the transport
equipment of the expedition consisted at first of a second-hand Ford
which we bought to enable us to get to and from Haifa, our base.
Then a small Ford lorry, for hauling out building materials, etc., was
purchased. Later a fine International truck generously presented by
Mr. Cyrus H. McCormick, of Chicago, was invaluable for heavy
haulage. At the gate is a small room for the guard. A long storage
room and a machine-shop were afterward built along the eastern side

FIG. 10.—Headquarters of the expedition. View northward with Nazareth and Tabor in the background

of this court (right side in Fig. 10). The small separate building next to it contains sleeping-rooms and shower bath for the native staff and a large office for the clerk of the works. Here the workmen are paid off each Thursday evening.

The main building extends along the northern side of the compound (far side in Fig. 10) and is entered by a door from the inner court. This admits to a large hall with doors opening respectively to the office, to a long hall connecting the various workrooms along the north side, and to the library and dining-room. At one side of it a stairway ascends to the second floor, where are the sleeping-rooms and a large living-room used also for cinema exhibitions and lectures. Along the court side on the lower floor a small room used for drawing the objects is fitted with cases for storing the smaller objects such as beads, flints, scarabs, etc., and a large steel file for the card index of all the data collected. Next to this comes the main registration and storage room. Along the window side of this room are work tables, and opposite these are shelves arranged like a library stack, for pottery, etc. Each shelf bears the number of the tomb or room to which the objects stored on it belong, and each stack of shelves has a projecting label showing the rooms or tombs represented in that stack. Beyond this room, at the eastern end of the building, is a large drafting-room fitted with three drawing tables with adjustable top lights, a storage cabinet for maps and plans, and space for all varieties of drawing instruments, paper, etc.

Along the north of the building and opening from the long hall is a series of smaller rooms: first a secretary's office, next a room for storing surveying instruments, then a toilet, and finally a large dark room. This room has been fitted up with every convenience for photographic work, and the pictorial results prove its value. It is a long room with three small square windows along the outside. Each window is fitted inside with a combination wooden shutter so designed that by lifting the upper flap daylight can be admitted, while smaller flaps in the lower half give a ruby, green, or other light needed at the moment for photographic developing. Under the windows a table extends the whole length of the room. It contains two sinks with running water, one sink having a filter attached. There are shelves for chemicals and storage of supplies, and at one end is an electric printing machine. We use cut films only, manipulated in wire frames, so that as soon as the film is exposed it may be transferred from the holder and held safely in one of these wire frames through all the processes of developing, fixing, washing, and drying, no hand actually touching the film until it is completely finished. The dark room is entered by a "staggered" or double-elbow passage which needs no door, but which insures both adequate ventilation and complete darkness, because all the walls of the passage as well as of the dark room itself are painted a matt black. At the northeast corner of the building, connecting with this dark room, we subsequently built a large studio with two large glass windows and a skylight, so that any required lighting can be obtained for photographing all varieties of objects. This department of the work always interests visitors, as it is a model of its kind.

All the outer walls, besides certain walls on the ground floor serving to tie the whole structure together, are of stone. A few subdivision walls here and all those on the upper floor are built of wooden studding covered with "sheetrock." This was donated by the United States Gypsum Company. Its use greatly facilitated the construction, while its soft gray color essentially improved the appearance, of the interior of the house. The entire plant is supplied with water from the Ain el-Kubbi just below the house (see map, Fig. 6). A cement-lined and roofed-in collecting tank was built behind the source of the spring so as to prevent its contamination by the natives or their animals. From this tank a pipe leads to a small automatic electric pump in a locked building a few meters above it. The pump works under pressure and keeps a constant supply of water in the house.

Extending along the western side of the inner court is the service wing (at left in Fig. 10). In this is first a storeroom for food supplies, then the power plant, in which are installed a Delco lighting outfit and a Frigidaire equipment. Adjoining this is a small pantry where the refrigerator is located, and next is the kitchen. The oil cooking range here, as well as most of the sleeping and living equipment of the expedition, was donated by Sears, Roebuck and Company. Beyond the kitchen is a sleeping-room for the house servants.

The fourth (south) side of the inner court (near side in Fig. 10) is occupied by an open shed divided into alcoves with shelves and racks. Here the pottery from the work is brought to be washed, sorted, and repaired before entering the registration rooms. The series of operations from the finding of the object to its final disposal on the storage shelves will be described later. Outside the rear of the compound is a long dormitory for the Egyptian *reises* (native foremen), with a separate room at one end for the head foreman. In the main building is installed a telephone connected with a booth on the top of the mound, in the midst of the excavations. This field booth can be moved around as the area under examination changes. This keeps those in the house in instant communication with the work.

Our staff included Mr. D. H. Higgins, engineer and geologist, assisted by Mr. E. L. DeLoach, to whom the careful contour map of the site (Fig. 11) is due. My nephew took charge of the financial end of the expedition until illness necessitated his leaving Palestine. Miss Ruby Woodley then looked after the accounts and assisted in the final registration of objects. Near the end of the first season we secured the services of Mr. Olaf Lind, a skilful photographer from Jerusalem, who is responsible for the beautiful photographs of the excavations and of pottery and other objects. Labib Effendi Sorial from Luxor acted as clerk of the works and also helped in measuring and drawing many of the sheets of the general plan and of the tombs. In this he was assisted by William Effendi Gad of Luxor. Both of these Egyptians had been trained by me. Egyptian workmen to the number of sixteen, all specially skilled in detecting floor levels, following out walls, and clearing graves, formed the nucleus of the main body of unskilled local labor.

In my original suggestions made to Dr. Breasted in regard to the expedition, I had proposed that our first season should be largely preliminary work. Of first importance was the establishment of our permanent quarters. Next was the preparation of an accurate map of the hill and its environs. This should be made before extensive excavations altered the form of the mound. To some extent the old work of 1903–5 had changed the uppermost levels, and these would have to be sketched in from a small map made at that time. In addition to all this, I hoped to get a great amount of preliminary excavation done, clearing the later, uninteresting levels out of the way, so that succeeding years could be devoted entirely to investigating the more important historical portions of the hill. In our first season we were able not only to accomplish the establishment of the permanent camp and the completion of a large map with contours at two-meter intervals, which will serve as the basis for aligning the sheets of the successive strata as they are completed, but we were able to uncover and record fully three separate strata over the eastern end of the summit. Furthermore, a considerable area on the eastern slope (cf. Fig. 38) was cleared, mapped, and then used for the great dumping ground of refuse from the summit. As a result of this advance clearance, not one meter of the archaeological area has been lost and no ground that has not first been thoroughly explored need be buried under an immense dump.

III

METHODS

The complete excavation of a large mound which contains many superimposed strata offers difficulties that do not obtain in a smaller site or in one that has but shallow accumulations of débris. As already mentioned, our knowledge of Megiddo indicated that it represented a long period of history. The problem set for us was to trace the character of this long period back to its origin, in so far as it was discernible in the remains preserved in the mound. We were to establish the chronological sequence of the various strata and link up each one with known names, facts, and dates which were available from outside sources. The plans, construction, and contents of the buildings and tombs of Megiddo were to be recorded and studied, in order that we might later be able, to a certain extent, to reconstruct the appearance and life of its people during each stage in the development of the city. Our fundamental principle was the collection of data for such reconstruction, instead of a mere accumulation of portable antiquities. These data had also to be classified and filed for ready reference.

On a totally unknown site it may sometimes be advisable to make a small preliminary sounding or run a trench into the heart of the hill, in order to determine just what periods may be represented in its mass and, if more than one layer becomes apparent, the character and age of each. In any case, such a vertical cutting must be abandoned as soon as it becomes evident that there are several levels to be dealt with, and before any extensive cutting-up of the strata has been done. At Megiddo the hill was cut up by test trenches, the main one 20 meters wide, 12 meters deep, and extending nearly across the hill. It went down through many different layers of buildings, only two of which were recorded; so its extent must in our plans of the different strata be represented by white paper. In the previous section we have seen how the hill was built up layer by layer. It should be obvious that the logical method of determining the extent of the respective remains of each separate town level and securing as complete a record as possible of its character, is to reverse the process and strip off layer after layer, beginning with the topmost or latest in date. The task is complicated by the fact that, instead of being nicely and evenly differentiated like the layers of a cake, the strata are rarely horizontal throughout and never parallel. Only the first habitations clustered on the perhaps nearly level original summit of the hill. Successive towns expanded over the edges, either following the natural slopes or built on artificial terraces. Narrow vertical cuttings would never indicate the intricacies of such constructions. By missing the determining factors beyond its limits, a trench might lead to quite erroneous conclusions.

It would be ideal to lay bare the entire extent of each building period; but in the case of a mound as great as that of Megiddo, Hazor, and similar sites, where questions of crops, ownership of lands, leases, and dumping areas enter in, it is not always practicable to do this. At Beth Shean the whole area of the later periods—early Arab, Byzantine, and Roman—was thus cleared over both the entire summit and also the lower terraces. At Samaria we had to devise another system. The summit was cleared in small areas, each stratum being excavated and recorded in its natural order. When one section was finished, the débris from the work in the adjoining area was thrown into it. The many thick walls found there made it imperative to leave as much as possible in position. Had the range of periods, however, been as great as at Megiddo, it would have been impossible to obtain satisfactory records of the lower levels without destroying most of these massive constructions. At Megiddo the area of the summit was more than 46,000 square meters, and to clear all of this level by level would entail long railway hauls and slow down the work to an undesirable extent. Fortunately, the old trench made a convenient boundary, since it would show in every level as a wide gap. So we chose the high portion east of this, where, according to the topography of the mound, must lie the main buildings of the city.

Apart from the preparation of the topographical survey, the field work may be divided into: (1) the actual processes of excavating, (2) the plotting of the walls and structures as they appear (cf. Fig. 16), (3) recording in detail the daily finds, and (4) photography. On the topographical map the whole site is divided into squares 25 meters on a side and oriented north and south (Fig. 11). These squares are pegged out over the area to be excavated. The corners are designated by letters and numbers in regular sequence, and references to any square are according to the number of its northeast peg, as R.13, etc.

When we are ready to begin work, squares are assigned by lot to the work gangs, of which we had three. This is to prevent jealousy, so that if one gang gets a square particularly rich from the workmen's point of view, that is, full of *antikas*, there will be no ill feeling among them, no notion that a good square has been picked for a favorite gang. Some of them believe that we know exactly what each square is going to contain. The squares are chosen in groups so as to concentrate the work and clear as great a space as possible at one time. Each gang has its own branch of railway, which was laid out in old trenches, converging toward the main dump, which will be explained later. At the end of each line is a siding, on which always stands in reserve an empty car, ready to be filled while its loaded fellow is on its way to the edge.

The actual superintendence of the work of the gangs is in the hands of the chief foreman, who keeps the people moving, watches that the limits of neither area nor stratum are exceeded, and sees that the railway works smoothly. Each gang is under a skilled foreman (*reis*), who has three or more equally trained Egyptian laborers under him, distributed among the local workpeople. A gang consists of pickmen, scrapers or basket-fillers, and a number of carriers. Women and girls, as well as men and boys, were used as carriers.

Where excavations have previously been made, the gangs simply proceed to complete the clearance of the rooms already partly visible, and even then only on the latest exposed level. On virgin areas the pickmen of the gang, usually numbering four or six selected men, work in line across the width of the square and away from the railhead. They break up the surface soil to a depth of about 30 cm. (Fig. 12). Behind them follow double the number of scrapers or fillers, who break up the clods of earth, carefully watching for fragments of pottery and other objects. After examining the earth, they load it into baskets and pass them to the long line of women, boys, and girls, who carry them to the waiting car. When one depth of earth has thus been removed, the pickmen return to their first positions and repeat the oper-

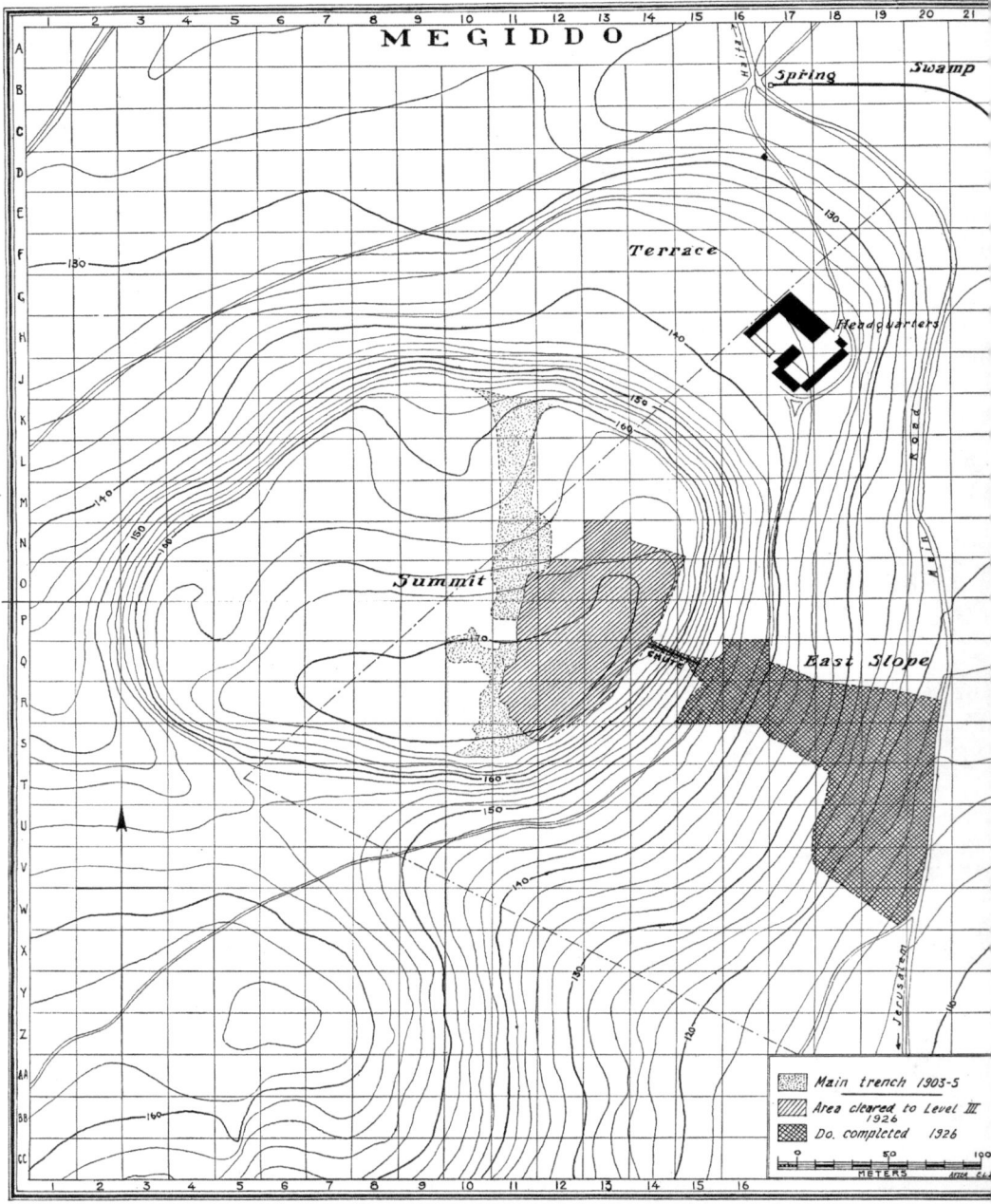

Fig. 11.—Contour map of Megiddo (DeLoach)

ation on another 30 cm. of soil. Any fragments of jars, handles, rims, and other objects are placed in baskets provided for that purpose at the edge of the work. These are tagged with their provenience number and are carried to the headquarters at the close of the day, or, if of unusual importance or value, at the noonday rest hour. This process continues until the tops of walls appear. Then the method is changed. The pickmen are distributed over the square and begin to

Fig. 12.—Pickmen breaking up the surface layer of earth

follow the walls down to a pavement level. Rooms at once receive regular numbers such as I 15, which would indicate that this room was the fifteenth found in the first or topmost stratum. Objects now found are given the room number and a serial number preceded by an x, as are also those found in the indefinite surface layers. This signifies that, while found in the area or room stated, they were not in position and therefore must be used with caution as evidence. Often, before the floor of a room is reached, jars, either singly or in groups, may be found. These are left *in situ* until the position is located on the plan and, if of special interest, a photograph is taken. No object, even in such a position, is ever moved until this record is complete.

When objects are found *in situ* on the actual floor, one of the
trained Egyptians is set to work with knife, fingers, bellows, and brush.
He slowly removes the earth from around them, leaving only enough
to sustain the objects in position. When large groups are thus found,
the position of each thing is drawn and indicated with a number
on a special larger-scale plan of the room. A detail photograph is
also taken, but this is usually omitted when it would add nothing

FIG. 13.—Scarp of unexcavated area seen from Stratum III, disclosing a vertical section of the two overlying strata. Some of Schumacher's dump above.

to our record. A series of rooms comprising a house is photographed
from a large wooden tripod 8 meters high, giving a bird's-eye view
over them. Figs. 39–43 are views taken in this manner. Each square
is excavated to the first floor level reached. When all its rooms
are cleared, the gang removes to another square, while the walls are
entered on a sheet of the general map. When one layer has been uncovered over the whole area chosen for excavation, some general
bird's-eye views, showing the relation of different buildings and
streets, are taken.

Then begins the search for the next period. The gangs return to
their original squares and first demolish the finished walls of the

stratum, level, or layer just excavated. The work then proceeds as in
the first case, except that usually the earlier walls appear immediately
below the later floors (cf. Fig. 13). If not, the thin peeling process is
resorted to again.

Thus level after level is found, thoroughly examined, and recorded
as though no other period were represented on the hill. Each becomes
quite simple and clear in turn. Such difficulties as re-use of walls, overlapping of levels, changes of floor levels in a long occupation, become
apparent as the work progresses. On a large cross-section sheet which
hangs in the drafting-room, the levels of the different superimposed
cities are drawn as they are ready. By this method one keeps in touch
with the historical sequence and feels tremendous satisfaction in seeing
the story of the hill develop.

Some squares require a longer time to clear than others; and in
order to prevent the clearance in one place from advancing faster than
in others, part of a gang is often withdrawn and shifted to other jobs.
Sometimes the outside task may be collecting stones for a new shed at
the headquarters or getting rid of an awkward heap of stones, but
more usually it is cemetery work. At Megiddo we may always expect
tombs on any of the slopes outside the city walls. The excavation of
a rock tomb follows somewhat the same procedure as just outlined,
except that its character is known as soon as an entrance is discovered.
Only a few men can find space for working, and an Egyptian is always
present. All tombs, except in those rare cases when we find one completely sealed, are full of débris and washed-in earth. This is cleared
stratum by stratum as in the case of a room, and the objects from the
different levels are carefully differentiated. The record is kept on a
5×8-inch card with millimeter ruling. A scale sketch is made of the
grave, and a description of size, character of grave and skeleton, and a
rough list of contents are written in beside it. Figure 14 shows a sample
record along with the photographic record. The débris from tombs and
from all important building levels, such as the floors of rooms, is run
through fine sieves by a keen-eyed Egyptian lad (Fig. 15). The
scarabs from Tomb 37, shown in part in Fig. 26, were salvaged in
this manner.

The general plan of the excavations is drawn to a scale of 1 : 100
on sheets each containing four of the squares shown on the topo-

graphical map and thus covering an area of 2,500 square meters. The name of the site and the number of the sheet are lettered in the upper left-hand corner. The squares are ruled in red. At the right a wide space is reserved for "Notes." Here are drawn details of masonry or sections showing overlapping of walls, with such other notes as may seem necessary to make clear peculiarities of construction. Black hatchings are used for the different materials, such as limestone rub-

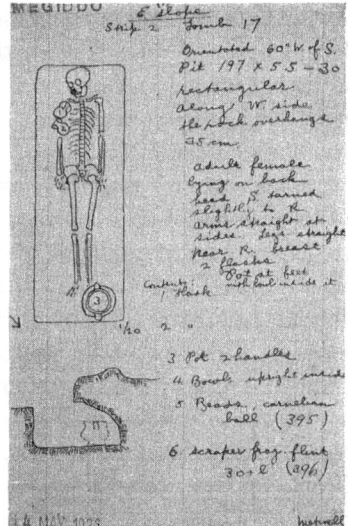

FIG. 14.—Tomb 17. At left, the photo record before removal of contents. At right, the record card of grave with list of objects. Other cards contain scale drawings and full descriptions of all objects.

ble, mud bricks, etc., while color washes indicate different periods. The Stone Age has stone-gray washes, the Bronze Age shades of brown and yellow, the Iron Age blues, while the later empires have purple, rose, and pale pink for the Hellenistic, Roman, and Byzantine periods respectively. The Arab and Crusader colors are greens. For all these a special chart has been prepared, covering all the possible ages in Palestine. Only the outlines of the various walls are first plotted. Then the sheets are handed to the detail man, who enters the details of stonework, pavements, etc. (Fig. 16). In addition to these sheets are the "Progress Cards," printed on white stock 5×8 inches in size.

One of these is made out for each room as soon as it appears; and day by day the progress of the work in that room is entered, with mention of characteristic objects found in its débris, its relation to other rooms, and its significance in the general scheme of that level. Another form, headed "Survey Card," contains all the data for completing the plans of the different rooms. All dimensions are entered on it, besides such rough sections, etc., as cannot readily be shown on the plans. From

FIG. 15.—Sifting débris from Tomb 37

these records the diary is made up. The general plan, the larger-scale drawings of special rooms, the sections, the various cards for progress, surveying, and record of objects, photographs of the site and of individual rooms, together make up a complete record of the work.

Let us now trace the course of objects found in the excavations from the time they are placed in the baskets on the edge of their area until they are ready for the division between the Palestine Museum and our own Oriental Institute Museum at Chicago. The tag which is attached to each basket contains spaces not only for a note of the area and particular room to which the group belongs, but also for a brief list of the contents arranged by material: pottery, stone, metals, glass, etc. At the right are three columns for checking off the completion of the three stages in the complete record of the objects found, viz.: drawing, registration, and photography; and there is also space for the date of the find and the designation of the gang which made the find.

FIG. 16.—Measuring up rooms on the summit. Stratum III (800–600 B.C.)

At the close of each day the heads of the gangs detail workers to carry down to the inner court of the house the baskets from their own gang. There the baskets are placed in groups to await their turn in the process of washing and sorting. One must remember that most of the pottery is found crushed by the weight of fallen walls and roofs (Fig. 17). At such a site as Megiddo there is an enormous quantity of fragments coming in each day, all of which have to be washed, sorted, and examined, since we must obtain not merely a record of the wares and a few shapes of rims and handles, but must endeavor as far as possible to reconstruct entire forms. This requires long and patient labor; but by giving to this portion of the work the proper care we were

able at Samaria, Beth Shean, and Megiddo to add many new shapes
to the corpus of Palestinian pottery.

FIG. 17.—A room on summit (800–600 B.C. level), showing collection of
pottery crushed by collapse of roof and walls.

The work-shed in the court is divided into five booths, and at the
entrance of each is affixed a label giving the provenience of each
separate group of pottery which is to be worked up. As the fragments
are washed, they are spread out on the shelves in their proper compart-

ment, a first sorting being made into groups of red, brown, or other wares. Decorated pieces are for convenience placed together. A native boy trained to this work now begins to search for pieces of the same vessel, fitting and gluing them together (Fig. 18). When finished as far as the fragments permit, each object is placed on the shelves to await the completion of the group. It often happens that we become crowded for space, and then each completed vessel is at once drawn to

FIG. 18.—Reconstructing a group of pottery forms

scale. The drawing is a sufficient record; and if the vessel is not a museum or study piece, it is discarded to make room for other shapes. Many duplicates occur in the course of excavations, and there are always odd fragments of broken jars which can never be assembled. Unless decorated, these are merely noted and then at once discarded.

The first registration room (Fig. 19) opens directly off the inner court. To it come all the objects from the excavations. As soon as they are found at the work, the small things such as hair pins, earrings, arrow heads, or scarabs are placed in small pill boxes, and then brought down with the baskets. They are at once removed for safety to this room and there await the completion of the repairs on the

accompanying pottery before being registered. As the repaired pottery comes in, each specimen is then drawn on a 5×8 card ruled in
millimeters. A special frame has been made to facilitate the work of
drawing them to scale. Ordinary sizes are made on a scale of 2 : 5,
while larger pieces, such as storage jars for wine and oil, are drawn 1 : 5
or even 1 : 10. Each card bears at the top the name of the site, the
provenience, and the period, and at the bottom the date when found

FIG. 19.—The first registration room. Drawing a stone grinding-bowl

and the gang number. In addition to the drawing of a pottery vessel,
a description is written beside or below it giving ware, details of decoration, if any, special features, and its dimensions in millimeters.
When the vessel has been thus recorded, the excavator may feel free to
decide whether it is to be kept or discarded. If it is retained, a space
between brackets is left just after the description for the proper note.
All the objects from one place are placed in shallow open trays together with the basket tag, on which in the column headed D (drawing) a check is made, showing that they have been through the drawing stage of the recording process. A number of these trays rest on a
wheeled rack, and when this has been filled it is rolled into the next
room (Fig. 20).

Here begins a new stage of recording, in which each object receives its sequence or registry number, and a copy of the drawing and description is entered in duplicate register books. The number is written either on the object itself or on a small tag attached to it. The registry number is also entered in the space left on the original millimeter card, and then the basket tag is checked off in the column R (registration).

FIG. 20.—The second registration room, with the storage cases

Thereupon the objects are ready for the photographic stage. The trays are now wheeled into the studio, where they are arranged in groups in order to photograph them against backgrounds of a tint suitable to their color. Bronzes, flints, ivories, and coins are photographed on a glass plate with a white ground some distance below it, so that they stand out clearly, without shadows around the edges to interfere with the contours. Pottery is photographed on a scale of 1 : 5 and other objects, as far as possible, full size. The operator makes identification notes regarding the positions of the various objects on the plate, before separating them. He also inserts a check on the tag in column P (photography), to show that he has completed his task. The trays of objects are then returned to the second room (Fig. 20), where they are placed on the storage shelves in regular order. Three prints are made from each negative. One remains in the photographer's file; another goes to the office file; and the third, with the photographer's notes on the position of the objects on the plate, is sent to the registration room. Here the registrar cuts it up and mounts the photograph of each individual specimen on a blue 5×8 card with the same provenience, date, etc., as on the respective object card. On both the latter and the blue card the negative number is written in blue ink.

The objects having now been completely recorded, all the 5×8 cards are returned to the first room, where they are arranged in steel files. Here also are filed all the progress and survey cards, so that when all the cards have been brought in, we find indicated by proper guide cards the complete data on any room or tomb: when and how it was cleared, a rough scale drawing of it, its contents drawn and described, and photographs showing the room with the objects in position as found and also after being cleared and reconstructed. If at any time the plans require to be consulted, they can be found in the large drafting-room next to the second registration room. They are there grouped stratum by stratum in portfolios in a large filing case.

It is upon this organized body of detailed information that the final full publication is based.

IV

CLEARING THE EASTERN SLOPE

The first task, before beginning the systematic dissection of the mound, was to provide a safe place for the immense amount of waste material that would result from the excavations. The disposal of such débris has always been an excavator's nightmare, and usually some area either on the edge of the proposed dig or even in its midst has been sacrificed for a dump. We had here an ideal hill, plenty of time at our disposal, and sufficient means to carry on our work properly; so I determined to put into practice a plan which I had long dreamed of trying out on a large site. After a survey of the different sides of the hill, I decided that the section along the east side, sloping down to the main road, which formed our eastern boundary, offered the most satisfactory conditions for the dump. On this side the central hill, which was presumed to represent the actual walled city in all its periods, sloped steeply down for about half its height, and below this began a series of gentle slopes and terraces representing the gradual accumulation of débris thrown and washed down from the summit and partly held by artificial retaining walls of modern date. At many points in its extent were rock outcrops, in nearly every case containing an opened tomb, so that we could be reasonably sure that this area was never within the occupation limits and that it contained no complicated strata. Actual results proved this hypothesis to be in the main correct, only isolated structures being found near the foot of the main slope.

A long trench was laid out on the slope, extending from the road to the portion of the summit edge chosen as the top of our dump. At the roadside a ledge of rock promised well for the easy clearance of the trench. Appearances, however, were deceptive; for after proceeding a few meters inside the road, we reached a deep quarry cutting parallel with it. It had partly destroyed the entrances to two rock tombs. These were the foretaste of an exasperating but productive area. With Tomb 1 we could not do much. It was in poor limestone

40

broken down by infiltration and criss-crossed with fissures due to earthquakes. This made it exceedingly difficult to work, and eventually we had to abandon following up the ramifications of the cavern because the lives of our people were endangered. It extended under the road and also northward beyond the limits set by our trench; and when in future the dumping area is increased in that direction, it can be traced more safely.

Tomb 2 was in better condition. Originally it had been entered by means of a vertical shaft, a feature common in early tombs; but the quarrying operations had left only the lower end of this intact. In the débris just outside of the entrance were several flint implements, saws and scrapers, none of them dating farther back than the Bronze Age. Types of the flints found in this area are shown in Figure 21. The interior of the chamber was filled to the top of the entrance with a fine silt washed in by many seasons of heavy rainfall when the door was still open to the sky. Below this was a stratum of coarser débris mixed with stone chips and containing numerous fragments of pottery with handles and rims, all much broken. Many of these could be reconstructed and proved to belong to a period toward the close of the late Bronze Age, 1300 B.C. There were abundant chisel marks on the walls and ceiling, and over the rocky floor was an irregular bed of limestone chippings. It appeared quite clear, therefore, that the original cavern might have been occupied as a dwelling as late as the early or middle Bronze Age. About 1300 B.C. it had been cleared out and enlarged, the roughness of the walls dressed down, and the cavern given a more regular shape. The mass of chips was spread over the floor to even up its irregularities. The cave was then used as a burial place, and the pottery scattered about by some later plunderers was all that was left of the funerary equipment.

The slope trench was divided into transverse strips, numbered and cleared in regular order from the road upward. As this work started before our contour map was completed, we could not utilize the square numbers; but survey positions were left on prominent points, from which the plan could later be adjusted to the general sheets. The two caverns just mentioned were the only ones in the first strip. In the next strip nothing was found but bare rock with portions of a rock water-channel with a slab covering.

In Strip 3 the rock was near the surface but was honeycombed with tombs. On the surface itself were the remains of a house containing

East Slope.
Strip 1, Area 3

FIG. 21.—Types of flint implements from eastern slope. All belong to the Bronze Age.

several small rooms and one large chamber with several square pillars supporting its roof (Fig. 22). Tomb 3, below this, was perhaps the most interesting of the whole series of burial places found in this vicinity. Its interior was in good condition and the débris was stratified in practically the same manner as in Tomb 2. There was the same top stratum of silt, the second of débris with potsherds, and the floor layer. The entrance was likewise through an outside shaft; and while the plan of the interior was irregular it had undoubtedly been adapted, as the tool marks showed, from an earlier and rougher cavern. Around

FIG. 22.—House on the eastern slope. The pillars supported its roof

the walls were niches for separate burials, and in the floor were several well-made circular pits nearly a meter in depth. All the pottery, etc., found was displaced and most of it broken. The plan and the pottery both showed that this and Tomb 2 were of the same date. Among the contents of Tomb 3 was a small bronze image of a Hittite warrior,[1] with shield in one hand and upraised ax in the other. Tombs 4 and 5 adjoined this one, breaking into it on the north. In Tomb 5 the entire roof had given way and had sunk into the chamber. In all these we came across fragments of the familiar milk bowls of Cypriote make, hemispherical in body, with wishbone handles, and decorated in bister with the usual ladder pattern. The houses were of much later date, as

[1] Or possibly a warrior god.—EDITOR.

FIG. 23.—Tomb 51, on the eastern slope, with door sealing and roof untouched. It was made about 1500 B.C., before the Hebrew occupation of Palestine.

FIG. 24.—Tomb 51 after the door had been opened and the roof removed

was also the heavy terrace wall found just behind them farther up the slope.

In the strip just at the foot of the steep slope work was stopped at the outer face of a heavy wall which I assumed to be one of the inclosing walls of the city. Outside this were groups of small rooms with rubble walls, and a few rock tombs. One of the latter, Tomb 51, is shown in Figure 23, after its exterior had been cleared. A walled pas-

FIG. 25.—Tomb 51. Interior, showing position of the pottery

sage led up to an entrance sealed with stones. The roof, of rough stone slabs, had partly collapsed and was held in place only by the mass of earth within the chamber. When the door was opened and the roof removed, the chamber was found filled with pottery (Fig. 24). A better idea of the contents is given by Figure 25, taken looking down through the open roof. This group belongs to a period not far from 1500 B.C., the pointed juglets and the small squat jugs of this date being prominent features of the collection.

When this slope trench had been nearly finished, an extension was begun along the road farther to the south. Ultimately this was joined up to the first one, when it was found necessary to increase the space

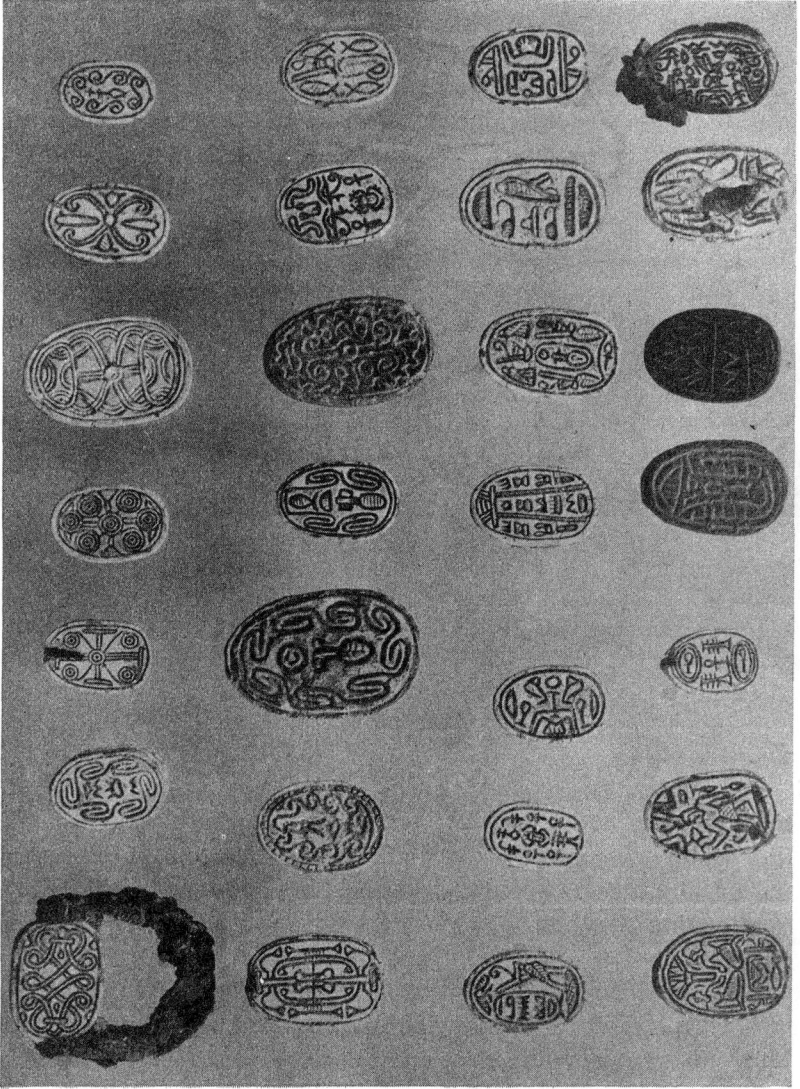

Fig. 26.—Egyptian scarabs from Tomb 37 (about 1700 B.C.)

for the rapidly growing dump. The new area proved more interesting and varied than the first strip. The portion adjoining the road was badly cut to pieces by quarries, which had destroyed the entrances and part of the plans of several tombs. One tomb here had been partly cleared in 1903. In extending its plan, our workmen broke through into an adjoining tomb, the real entrance to which appeared to come out under the road. This tomb contained Bronze Age pottery of 2500 B.C., similar to that shown in Figure 33, which was thrown out from a re-used tomb higher up to the west. At another point were found several large water jars lying in what seemed to be a much ruined grave. The tomb apparently extended farther into the hill; but as this would be in our second strip, we waited until the work reached it, as it is a rule never to break over the interior division lines of the work, except when a tomb develops at the limits of the area.

When we did come opposite to this spot in clearing the adjoining strip, we found a large tomb, its walls broken down to within a few centimeters of the floor. Its entrance was through a small round door at the bottom of a shaft. This led to a chamber nearly circular in plan. There were two side alcoves, and possibly a third had existed on the west, where the usual quarry had gone down below the floor level. The group of pottery first found belonged not to this tomb but to a partial re-use of one of its side alcoves. The later entrance had cut into this; and the remainder of the tomb, probably already packed with earth, appears to have been left undisturbed at this time, to be looted later by the quarrymen. The later burial belonged to the Iron Age, 600 B.C., but the original tomb contained a great quantity of pottery and other objects of 1700–1600 B.C. They were imbedded in débris which had been compacted by water and by the collapse of the roof into a layer as hard as rock. Days of slow and careful knife work on the part of our best Egyptian workman produced fragments which after washing and fitting gave us nearly a hundred shapes of jars, bowls, etc. Among these were a nearly complete jug of black ware with white-filled incisions, several beautiful polished red jugs, and others of extreme value and interest. In addition there were an ivory cosmetic box in the form of a duck, some bronze hair pins, and a splendid collection of scarabs (Fig. 26). The latter, mainly of Hyksos types, helped to confirm the date of the group of pottery. The finding of a

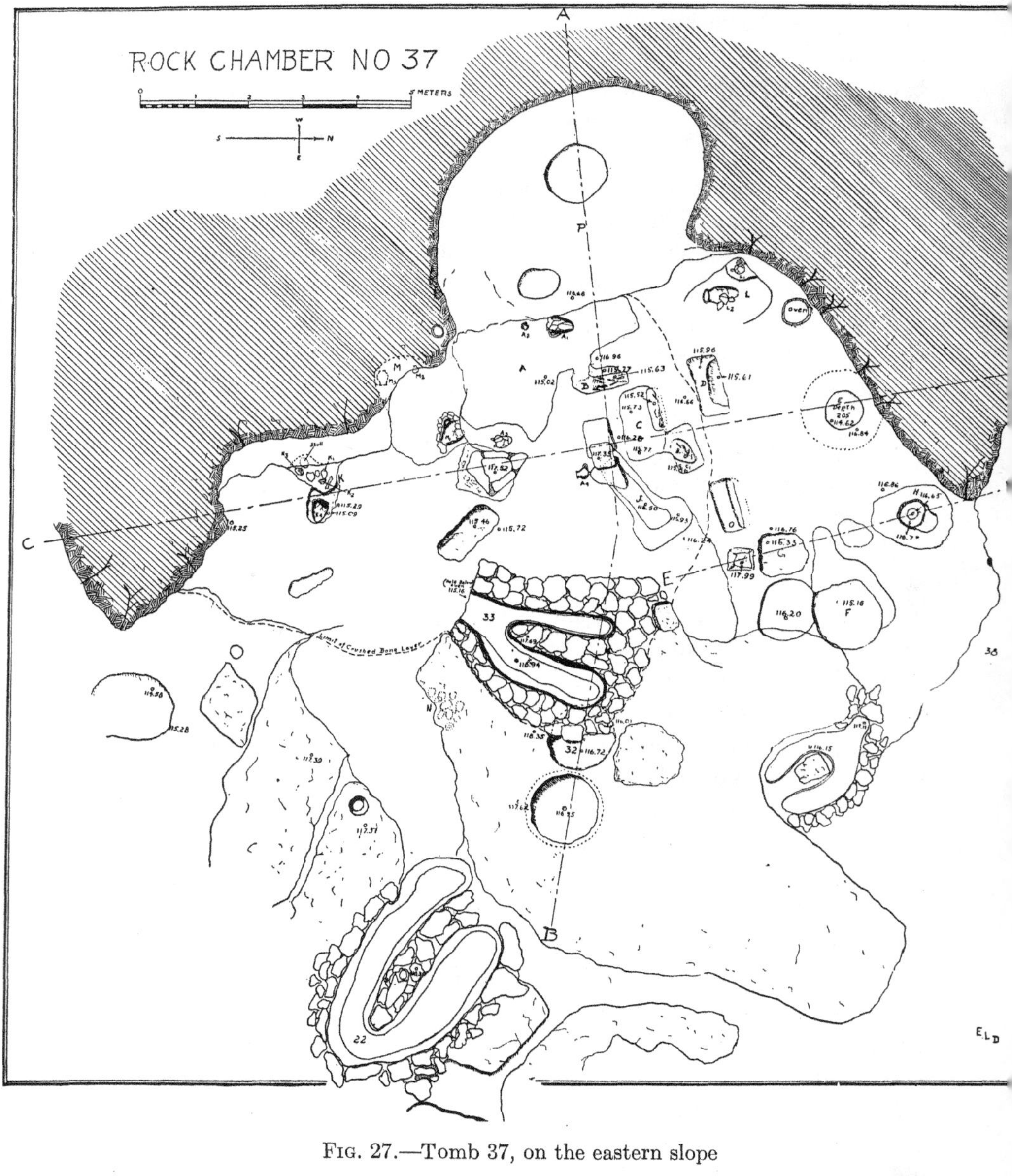

FIG. 27.—Tomb 37, on the eastern slope

tomb like this, hopeless as it looked at the first glance, when nothing but a mass of broken shards appeared buried in the earth, is one of the real fascinations of archaeological field work.

Apart from this rock tomb the most important was the huge dilapidated cavern numbered 37 (Fig. 27). The entire roof of this had collapsed, and we had to break up the many large pieces before we could move them away. It is quite possible that Tomb 37 was really a group of caverns which the destruction of the division walls had thrown into one. As found, the exact plan and the original height were lost. Probably the original entrance was somewhere near the left side, and the limits of the central cavern might have been as shown by the dotted lines. The large alcove at the rear would have been one of the main burial places, thus making the tomb resemble others found in its neighborhood. This curious place had a long and interesting history. In its rocky floor were several small scooped-out pits with a large jar in each containing the skeleton of an infant curled up inside. Either the top or the side of each jar had been broken to make it easier to insert the tiny body. None of the infants was more than a year old. One of these infant burials is shown in Figure 28. Beside the body are the jars containing its little supply of food and drink.

Within the limits shown by dotted lines on the plan (Fig. 27), the floor was much lower than in the rest of the cave, and this entire depression was filled to a depth of half a meter with splinters and fragments of partly burned bones. These probably represented the refuse from sacrifices to Astarte on the summit, and the cave was simply the depository for them between 800 and 600 B.C. The child burials belong to the later Bronze Age. At a much later period, the floor of the cave was leveled off roughly with earth and the place was then used for the manufacture of pottery. At H, near the right side of the plan, was a shallow work pit with a much worn stone socket inlaid in a rock pedestal in its center. In this the wooden potter's wheel revolved. There were also deep basins for water, and several of these were found filled to the top with a mass of potsherds. Outside the limits of the cave (see plan, Fig. 27) were three curious U-shaped structures identified as kilns (Fig. 29), resembling those used elsewhere as late as the Byzantine period. That one of these (No. 33 on the plan) was erected subsequent to the collapse of the roof is clear-

ly shown by its being built across a circular cup like many found over
the upper surface of the rock where it was still *in situ*. Another kiln
(No. 22 in Fig. 27) was found packed with pottery jar stands in a
partly baked condition. The doors of these kilns were in the curve
of the U and the pottery was stacked in the two legs. The interiors

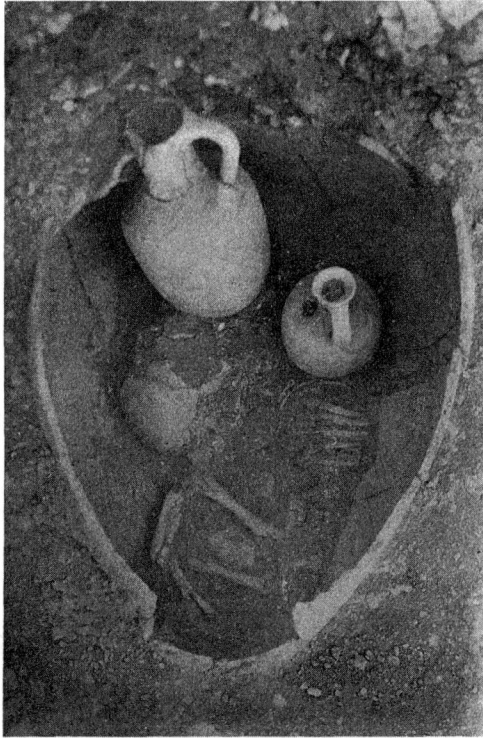

FIG. 28.—Jar burial of an infant in Tomb 37

were coated with a thick layer of mud, and the roofs were probably
of rough rubble. There must have been orifices for the exit of the
smoke from both ends of the U; but in still another, better-preserved
example found near by, there was a connecting vent between the ends
of the U which led to a single outlet. In the surrounding débris here
and elsewhere we found quite a number of potsherds cut to an elliptical
or eye shape. The edges were well worn and there was usually, but not

always, a hole for suspension. It may well be that these were scrapers or fashioning tools used by the potter, just as many of the crude saw-edged flints and the flint scrapers were used in an earlier period for a similar purpose.

The southern portion of the slope trench showed more than elsewhere the tremendous honeycombing of caves, which had left so little support in the soft limestone that some heavy earthquake had brought

FIG. 29.—Pottery kiln on eastern slope

down the entire mass. In Figure 30 this collapse is best seen. Just how many tombs were buried by this fall we cannot say. The greater portion of the earth below them has been examined and nothing found, and the removal of the entire mass would require an immense amount of labor. In the rear of this picture can be seen the entrance to Tomb 39. The fall of rock had cut in half its vertical shaft. Figure 31 gives a plan and section of this tomb after it was cleared, while Figure 32 is a view of the interior taken through the low door, showing the contents in position. The roof of this tomb was dangerously cracked, so it had to be shored up while we were working and until the drawings and photographs had been made and the objects safely removed. The pottery group was remarkably fine, with a considerable number of

FIG. 30.—South end of lower slope, showing collapse of surface rock into tombs

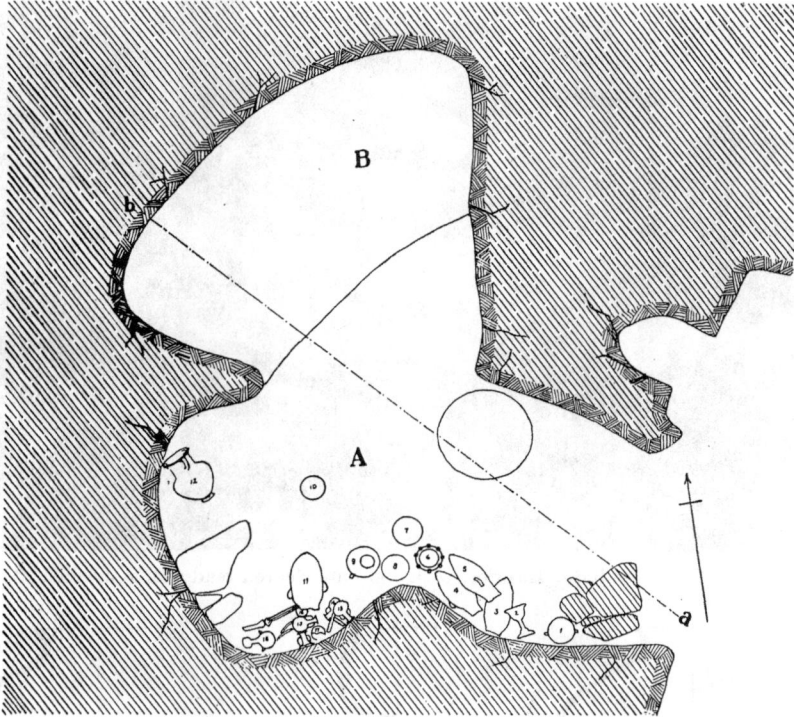

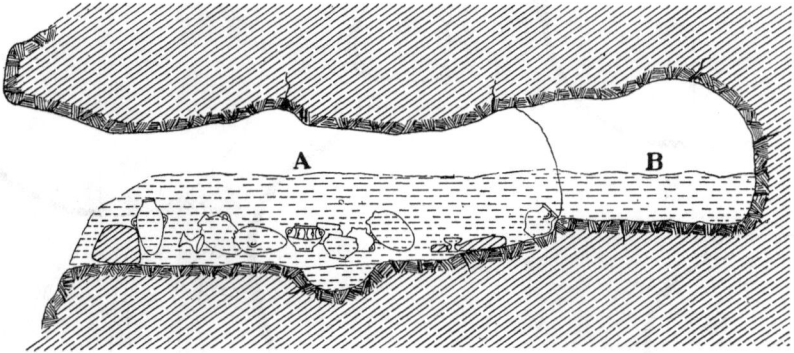

SCALE ━━━━━━━━━━━━━━━━━━━━ METRES

Fig. 31.—Tomb 39. Plan and section

FIG. 32.—Tomb 39. Interior, with contents cleared ready for recording

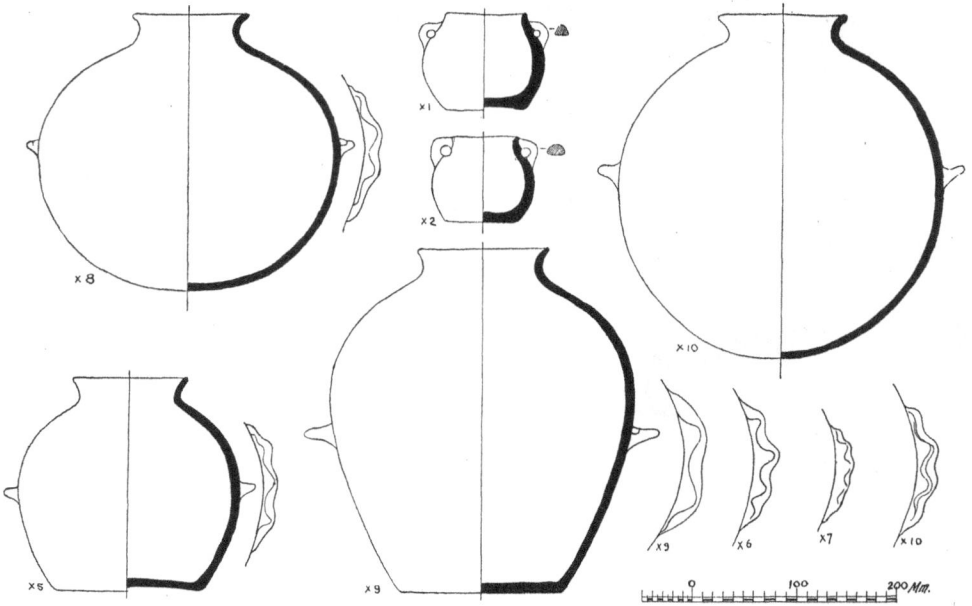

FIG. 33.—Forms of Bronze Age pottery from Tomb 16 (about 2300 B.C.)

different shapes linked up together as belonging to about 1000 B.C. Besides several large jars, there were two bowls with tall pedestal bases, of the type sometimes called chalices. The finest piece was an eight-

FIG. 34.—Tomb 19, with three disturbed bodies and objects

handled pot with red decoration, to be seen nearly in the center of the picture. Besides these there were several gold earrings and other ornaments and some gold foil. A number of additional vessels not actually *in situ* on the floor were taken from the loose débris. The tomb was remarkable because so many of these specimens were intact, which was certainly not the condition of most of the pottery from the eastern slope.

Although the isolated tombs and chambers on the east slope did not supply any related sequence of objects, they did provide evidence of the immense range in the history of the hill. For example Tomb 16, a much damaged tomb down near the modern road, produced quite an interesting group of early Bronze Age pottery. There were several

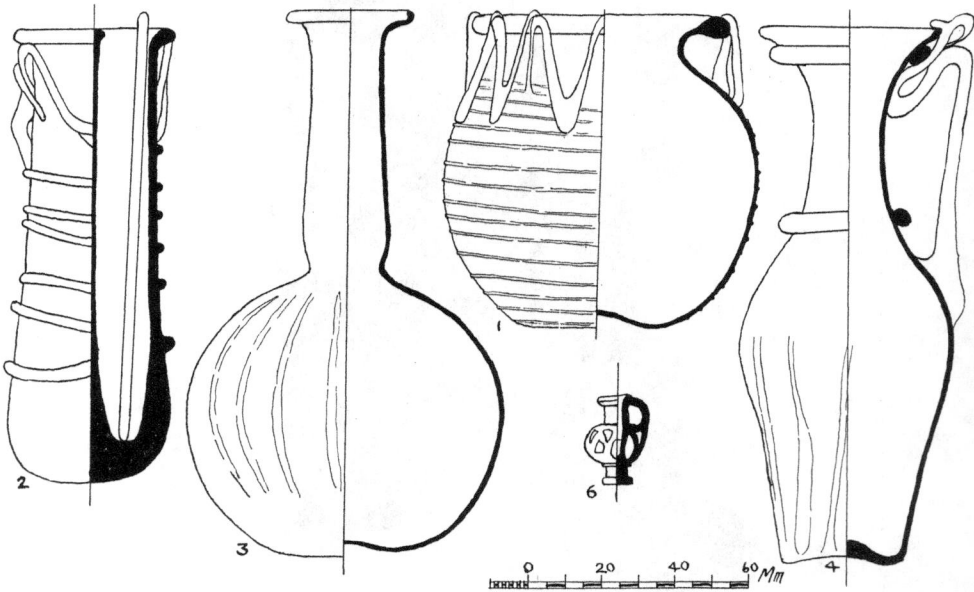

FIG. 35.—Glass from Tomb 19 (about 400 A.D.)

medium-sized storage jars, with both flat and round bottoms, and all with ledge handles (Fig. 33). The presence of the round-bottomed variety tends to place this group toward the end rather than near the beginning of the period, i.e. about 2300 B.C. All were handmade, and the two little pots x 1 and x 2 were quite characteristic. Not far from this was Tomb 19, which belonged at the very opposite end of Megiddo's history, the Roman period, about 400 A.D., when Roman influences were merging definitely into Byzantine. This was a rectangular grave in the débris, lined and roofed with slabs probably torn up from some more ancient floor. It had been used in two periods. The earlier consisted of the three burials shown in Figure 34 lying side by side with a black basalt grinding-basin and a group of glass vases at their feet. Later a single body was laid on top of these, with its head on the basin and its feet toward the east over the heads of the earlier interments. The collection of glass from this grave is shown in Figure 35. No. 1 was a globular pot of pale greenish glass, thinly blown and with a fine thread spun spirally around it. From the rim to the shoulder were draped rough festoons of thicker glass. No. 2 was a double tube used for keeping the *kohl* or black paint that still takes the place of rouge and lipstick in an oriental lady's facial adornment. In fact, inside it still remained the ivory stick with which the fair owner had applied the *kohl* to her eyelids. No. 3 was a plain greenish vase; Nos. 4 and 5 were of a more unusual type with fluted sides and graceful handle. In the débris between the basalt basin and the larger vases were two miniature vases of beautiful deep blue, with a network ornament over the sides and with tiny handles. One of these is shown as No. 6. They were only 25 millimeters high.

Just below this tomb and cut out of the rock below the stratum of débris in which Tomb 19 was built, was a shallow pit, No. 17, containing a middle-aged woman with a funerary outfit of pottery (Fig. 14). Near her neck were several decorated flasks for holy water. At her feet was a large two-handled pot to hold sufficient food for her trip into the unknown, and inside this was a small bronze bowl. Plunderers had removed everything which seemed to them of intrinsic value and had left only a single bead from her necklace, but fortunately all the pottery vessels. These belonged to the Iron Age, about 1000 B.C. Thus within a comparatively narrow area we had three distinct periods represented, which the finds on the regularly stratified summit will enable us to date by analogy within narrower limits.

V

EXCAVATION OF THE SUMMIT

Such in the main were the results of the large incidental clearance on the eastern slope, made primarily to insure investigated space for the dump from the excavations to be undertaken on the summit. We could now proceed to arrange for the disposal of the summit débris. An old German trench which extended well into the summit near the center of the east side had been chosen for the main axis of our railway system. Down the slope of the hill, in continuation of this axis, a trench about 2 meters wide was cut to the top of the already completed clearance on the east slope. A number of wooden sections were made, each 4 meters long and a meter wide, slightly tapering so that they could be fitted end to end. These were laid in the trench to form a chute (Fig. 36). At the top a section with spreading sides was fitted as a sort of hopper to receive the débris as it was dumped from the cars. At the bottom the end of the chute just cleared the top of a filled car, and a sliding wooden barrier was fitted here to regulate the loading. A single line of rails was laid under the foot of the chute (Fig. 37), but at a distance of several meters this branched into two parallel lines, which gradually extended toward the east as the dump heap grew (Fig. 38). This enabled several empty cars to be kept waiting, ready to be moved in and pushed under the chute as soon as a loaded car had moved out. At the top were two lines, one on each side of the hopper, coming from different areas of work. This chute served its purpose admirably. Slight delays occurred when two cars reached the top together and one had to wait until another empty could be pushed into place below. Tie-ups occurred when loaded cars on the lower dump line jumped the track, but after a few accidents of this sort we had the car men push the derailed car completely out of the way until the rest hour permitted its readjustment.

Work was begun on the three squares adjoining the top of the chute. Over the eastern part of the summit a number of rooms were already partly exposed, representing three separate periods. Some

58

walls had been removed during the former excavations, and others
had been partly destroyed by the network of trenches. Ignoring for

Fig. 36.—The wooden refuse chute, seen from the summit. The dump heap
spreads out over the cleared area below, where the tombs, etc., of Figs. 21–35 had
previously been excavated.

the time all the earlier periods exposed, I instructed our workmen to
remove first the old dump heaps on the top and then clear down to the
latest occupation floor level. There were no portable objects and no

pottery *in situ* to determine the dating of this final level of occupation, but such objects as were found in the débris indicated a date about

Fig. 37.—The lower end of the wooden chute, with a loaded car ready to be wheeled out upon the dump.

350 B.C. as the time of its destruction. The fragment of the Shishak stela (Fig. 7) came from one of the old surface dump heaps near the

eastern edge. The original stela had been broken up and its fragments used for building-stones for a building subsequent to 930 B.C. If it had been found in a wall it would have determined one possible limit of date for the building. Thus while interesting as proving the presence of Shishak at Megiddo, it does not have any stratigraphical value.

During its last two periods (Strata I and II) the hill was a mere fortified post along the highway and not a great walled-in city. In

Fig. 38.—The dump creeping out over the excavated tombs on the east slope. The projecting tracks are seen at the tip-off on the end of the dump.

both these levels the chief feature was a large fortress near the eastern edge, with the houses of an otherwise unprotected village behind it. The town plan was intersected by narrow, winding lanes, and it must have appeared much like one of the many modern Arab villages nestling on the summits or slopes of hills all over Palestine. The final period was much poorer in both house construction and general layout than the preceding one. The fortress still retained its main features, a rectangular building with an extension toward the south. Some of the earlier walls were used as foundations, but its area was contracted. The entrance was apparently on the west, as a narrow paved roadway led into it from this side. The outlying houses were of poor rubble

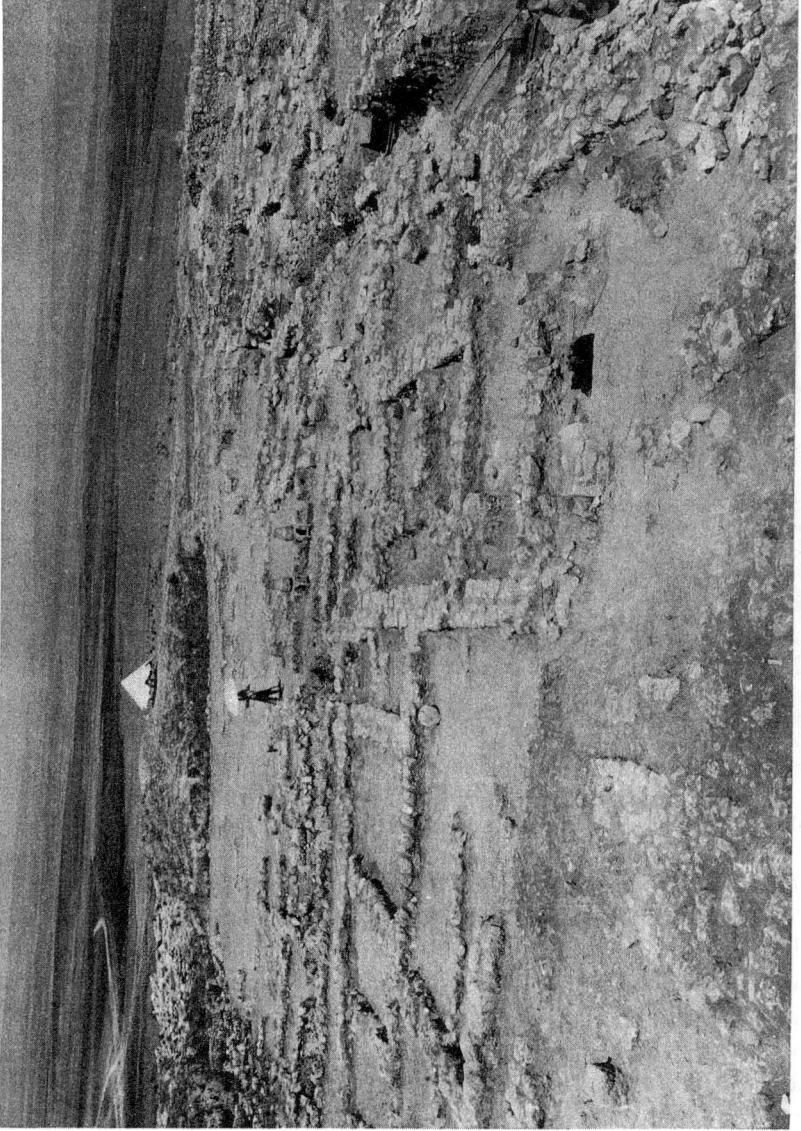

FIG. 39.—A portion of the latest stratum on the summit, lying between two trenches dug in 1903–5. The one at right is being used for our railway. At the extreme right are portions of the latest fortress walls.

construction, but toward the south were several more imposing structures with thicker and better-built walls (Fig. 39). One at least of

FIG. 40.—The summit, southern half, looking south. Clearing the topmost or latest series of houses, those of Stratum I. See our railway at left.

these had remained over from Stratum II. In Figure 40 is shown the
excavated area on the southern end of the summit, with the houses of
Stratum I. On either side of the railway are portions of the late fort

Fig. 41.—Walls of the late fortress in Stratum II

Fig. 42.—Northwest corner of the "Astarte Temple," showing the later fortress walls and the plastered bottom of a cistern built over the earlier masonry.

walls. In Figure 41 are the walls of the first or main fortress, with all later reconstructions removed. The fort of this period was quite a

FIG. 43.—The "Astarte Temple" in Stratum III

respectable affair. Portions of it had been removed in 1903, but it appears to have had three main divisions or courts, with barracks, stables, etc., around them. Of these courts, two were still traceable. On the north side was the main gate, with large, well-dressed stone jambs. This was at the inner end of a strongly walled passage, so that the entrance was well defended. The main walls were faced with roughly squared stones, with the interstices filled with small pieces, while the cores were simply rough rubble. Figure 42 shows how the walls of the preceding level were disregarded and the fortress walls built over and around what remained of the temple in Stratum III.

FIG. 44.—Rooms 6 and 7 of Stratum III (800–600 B.C.) with pottery *in situ*

At the right is seen the plastered bottom of the circular fortress cistern built partly upon the north wall of the temple.

The latest of these two periods lay so near the surface that at most only a course or two of masonry remained and the walls of many houses had disappeared altogether, having been plowed up in Arab times and the stones used for field walls. The top stratum, therefore, represented Megiddo in its last phase. With the ultimate passing of this village, even the name of the old town was lost, and the hill was wholly abandoned as a building site. In the southern end was found one solitary tomb of the late Roman or Byzantine period, built into the ruins of a Stratum I house. This was the only remains of a period later than 350 B.C. thus far found on the summit itself.

Stratum II likewise contained but few objects from which to establish a date, but the stratum immediately below was clearly as late

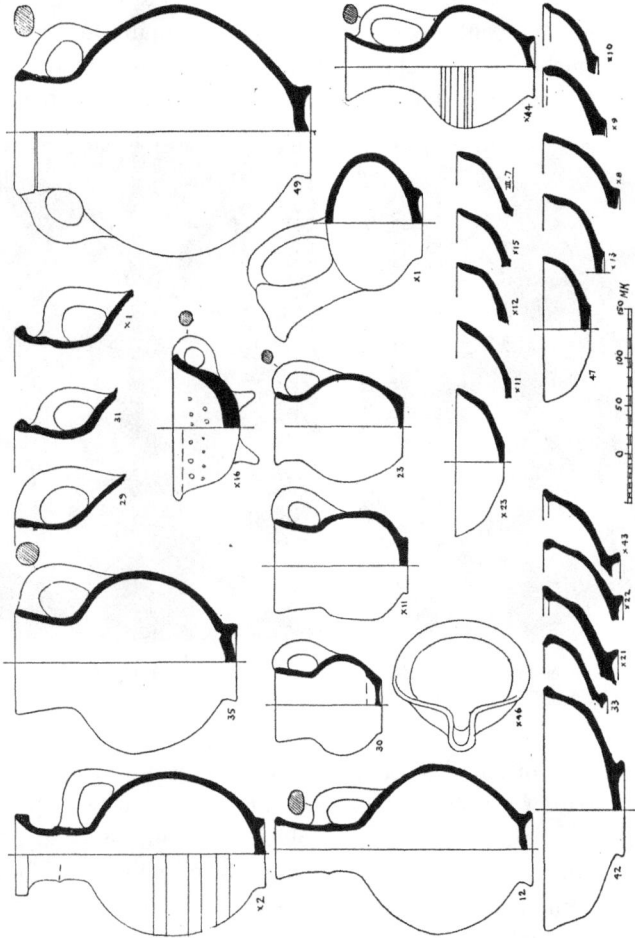

FIG. 45.—Selected forms of jugs and bowls from Rooms 6 and 7 of Stratum III (800–600 B.C.)

as 600 B.C. The second period was more pretentious in plan and the houses were better built. The streets were paved with rubble and many had shallow covered drainage gutters down the centers, features entirely lacking in the final, poorer town. We have no evidence what-

ever that the town itself in this period also was surrounded by any sort
of defensive wall.

The third stratum brings us down to 800–600 B.C. On this side
of the summit were a number of rooms clearly belonging to a large
single group. This I assumed to be a temple of Astarte (Fig. 43). The
entire complex has not been cleared, but its main feature was a
more finely finished central shrine, its foundations being the old walls
of an Israelite building. This stood in a large court, which was sur-

FIG. 46.—Three stone altars from
the "Astarte Temple."

FIG. 47.—One of the "Astarte
Temple" altars after repairs, showing
its four horns.

rounded by rows of small apartments and larger storerooms. These
were built partly of rubble and partly of large mud bricks. The bricks
corresponded in size to the well-cut blocks of stone used in a thick
recessed wall which apparently encircled the whole summit. The inner
walls of the temple complex were oriented in agreement with this
inclosing wall, which, although possibly of an earlier date, was still
a feature of the city in the temple period. Between the inner face of
this wall and the temple building was a space several meters wide
which continued uniformly as far as it was followed. It was crossed
only by the house walls of Strata I and II. In several of the storage

rooms were large quantities of pottery crushed in position by the collapse of the building (cf. Fig. 17). Another long storeroom is shown in Figure 44. Here was a collection of all sorts of vessels, large jars

FIG. 48.—Incense altar (35 cm. high) from the "Astarte Temple"

filled with burned grain, and many jugs and bowls. A selection of these is shown in Figure 45. All these lay in a shallow bed of ashes, and all bore traces of great heat, such that the bands of red and black on the decorated pieces were often nearly obliterated. These signs of the severe conflagration which had destroyed the building were traceable throughout all its rooms. The black traces were on the top of the fine Israelite masonry, but not upon the sides, showing that at this period it was below the floor level and had been merely re-used as foundations and did not form part of the temple superstructure.

FIG. 49.—Figurine of Astarte

Just south of the long storeroom (Fig. 44) full of pottery, and apparently outside the boundary of the complex, were found three limestone altars, badly split up into fragments by heat (Fig. 46). Two of these had horns at the four upper corners (Fig. 47), and the other had a top resembling a seat. Near by were fragments of two terra-cotta incense altars, representing shrines with windows. One had animal figures on the sides and heads of Astarte at the front upper corners (Fig. 48); the other was smaller and simpler. Possibly they belonged together, forming a two-storied model of a temple. These with the three stone altars had evidently been carried out of the building and broken up when the temple was looted and burned. Several figures of Astarte were found on the summit and on the eastern slope. The best preserved is shown in Figure 49. In the débris of this level have been found three capitals for square piers (Fig. 50). One of these lay near

FIG. 50.—A capital from the "Astarte Temple"

the altars, another was built into the fortress wall of Stratum II, and a third is recorded as having been found in a wall removed during the excavations of 1903.

All the pottery found in the burned rooms belongs to the Hebrew period; and the capitals, which evidently formed part of the structural decoration of the central shrine, are Cypriote in origin and date between 800 and 600 B.C. Thus Stratum III represents a time when the Hebrews, during one of their lapses from the worship of Jehovah, gave their allegiance to Astarte.

The Astarte level is the lowest which was systematically traced in the first season. Only below the level of the temple have walls of the earlier Hebrew structure been exposed (Fig. 51). In this structure the masonry is quite different from that in any of the later strata. The

Fig. 51.—Walls of the Hebrew period, re-used in the "Astarte Temple"

blocks are much larger and have been laid with care so as to form a firm bonding in the wall. The superstructure, of which several courses are shown in Figure 52, is beautifully dressed and fitted and parallels exactly the masonry from the Omri and Ahab palaces found at Samaria. In 1903 there were found on the southern edge of the summit the remains of a large hall and portions of the walls of a court, which are also certainly Israelite. These may be part of the reconstruction of

Fig. 52.—The southeast corner of the Israelite structure, period of Ahab

Megiddo during the reign of Solomon, whose masonry would not differ materially from that of the Samaria palace, so that we may have here still another stage in the occupation of the hill. It would have been this earlier structure that was destroyed by Shishak about 926 B.C. Further excavation, however, may connect this building with that on the eastern edge and thus bring the reconstruction of the building on the summit as an Astarte temple down to the Ahab period. The pottery found in the latter structure would be against this, and the more plausible theory would be that the southern building is Solomonic and the upper one of Ahab's time (874–835 B.C.). The latter was destroyed and its walls used as foundations for the Astarte building between 700 and 600 B.C., and the final temple was burned sometime after this date. This, with the two subsequent fortress periods, gives us a consistent sequence of dates for the strata thus far exposed.

VI

THE POTTERY CORPUS

In carrying on excavations either in Palestine or in Egypt it has always been difficult to compare objects from the various expeditions. In the published volumes of archaeological material, pottery, for example, is rarely adequately and uniformly described and illustrated, although it has become recognized that pottery is our main clue to the dating of strata.

In order that any corpus of pottery may be completely useful, it should contain information on the following points in connection with every type of vessel: (1) its form, including the interior structure; (2) its finish; (3) its decoration; (4) the material of which it is made, including, if possible, an analysis of the ware; (5) the method of its manufacture, especially whether made by hand or with the wheel; (6) its period and its place in the development of a particular form; (7) its distribution throughout the country; (8) the influences, either local or from other countries, which have produced or changed its form and decoration.

These data should be classified so that any one can look up as quickly as possible the group of vessels belonging to any particular period, the period or periods in which any form or its variations are to be found, the various types or forms, the wares and varieties of decoration. In short, given a fragment of pottery large enough to suggest the form, the ware, or the decoration, it should be possible to run down its type and assign the specimen to its proper place in the general scheme. The arrangement of material should be based on some definite expansive system, so that space is provided for entering new forms as they appear; for, Palestinian archaeology being yet in its infancy, many additional forms will of course be brought to light by future excavations. The aim of the present corpus is to bring together all the known types of Palestinian pottery into some such practical system.

Some years ago I prepared special cards for tabulating all the available data on pottery. A sample of one of these cards is given in Figure 53. The cards are of white stock, 8×10 inches in size, and are filed vertically. At the top are spaces for general data, such as the proveni-

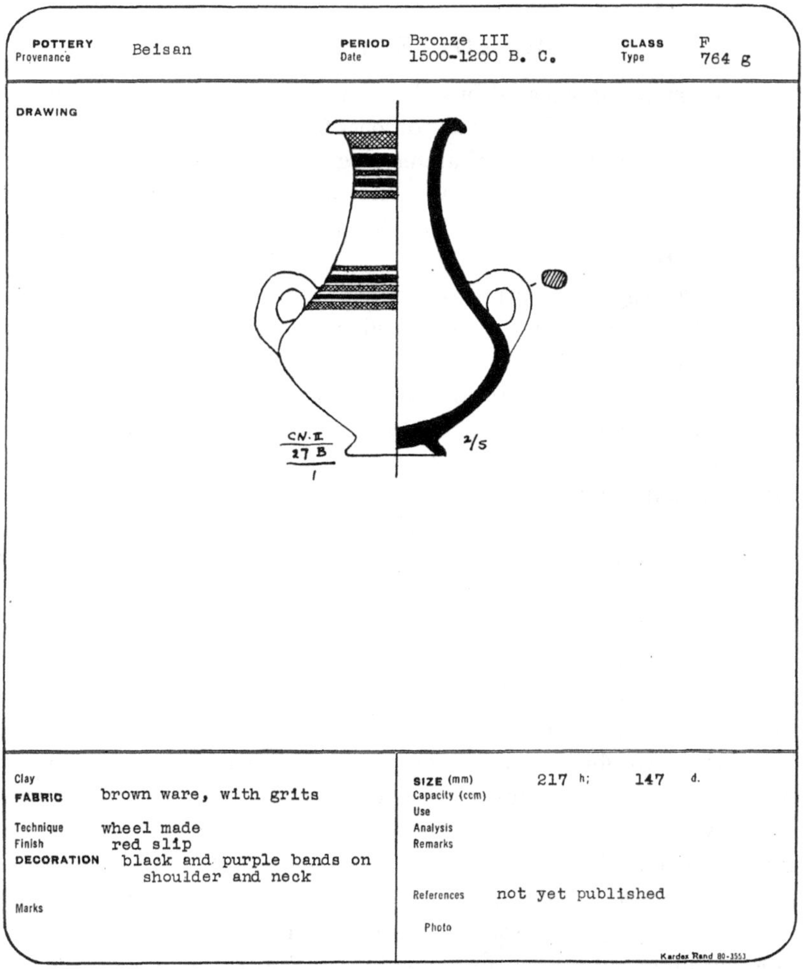
POTTERY Provenance: Beisan
PERIOD Date: Bronze III 1500-1200 B. C.
CLASS Type: F 764 g
DRAWING
CN·II 27 B / 1
2/5
Clay FABRIC: brown ware, with grits
Technique: wheel made
Finish: red slip
DECORATION: black and purple bands on shoulder and neck
Marks
SIZE (mm): 217 h; 147 d.
Capacity (ccm)
Use
Analysis
Remarks
References: not yet published
Photo
Kardex Rand 80-3553

FIG. 53.—Sample of record card for corpus of Palestinian pottery

ence of the specimen, its period, and its date. At the right is a space for the classification numbers. The main portion of the card is reserved for a scale drawing of the jar or bowl. For the ordinary-sized vessel, a uniform scale of 2:5 has been adopted, as that is large enough to show details of rim, base, or decoration and can be reduced one-half for publication. Large storage jars, on the other hand, which rarely have intricate details or decoration, are drawn to a scale of 1:5 or even 1:10. Details of finish, such as comb-facing, potters' marks, or motifs of decoration, are drawn to full size either on the same card or on separate cards which are marked with the same headings and filed immediately after the form card. In the lower left division there are spaces for more specific information, such as the clay used, fabric, technique, finish, decoration, and marks. On the right are spaces for the height and diameter in millimeters, the capacity when this can be obtained, the probable use of the vessel, a reference to the analysis of its ware, remarks on special or unusual features of the drawing, and references to the source whence the description and drawing were obtained and to a photograph if any has been published.

There is another card of the same size but made of pale green stock, on which an outline map of Palestine has been printed. On this in red ink can be indicated the various sites where each form of vessel has thus far been found. Such cards are placed after the white cards. Their object is to show at a glance the localities where certain forms seem to concentrate. Of course the value of this series grows with each excavation. Ultimately we can determine from our green cards the probable sources of origin of the various types and the routes by which they entered and spread through the country or whether they are products of certain districts only. This card provides space also for notes on clay beds and geological formations which will serve to indicate the place of manufacture.

When photographs of the various types can be obtained they are mounted on pale blue cards, and all historical data are noted on pale red. Through all our records this system of colors is adhered to: white for the general data, green for geography, blue for photography, and pink for history.

Already some 1,800 cards have been prepared, covering the types of pottery thus far excavated in Palestine. In many cases full information on all the points detailed above has not been available, but the increasing care and method with which excavations are being conducted will provide us with sufficient analogous forms to fill in the lacunae. This lack does not interfere in any way with the general scheme of classification. The whole mass of pottery forms is divided first into classes—large storage jars, portable jars, small jars, pots, bowls, jugs, etc.—designated by letters. After the various forms have all been redrawn to the uniform corpus scale from all the different sources and publications, they are sorted out into these main classes, dates being ignored for the moment. Under each class they are subdivided into types according to their form. Word descriptions have been entirely abandoned in designating this subgrouping. Instead, a three-figure number is assigned to each type. The first figure indicates the general shape, the second the shape of base or bottom, and the third that of the rim. All attachments, such as varieties of handles and spouts, have a letter which follows this number. Now bowls are classed under G, 0 has been adopted as the indication of roundness, and the wishbone handle is v in the list of handle types. Thus a Cypriote milk bowl, which is about as simple a form as one can obtain, with a round body, round bottom, plain, rounded rim, and wishbone handle, would have the class designation G, with 000 as its type number and v added for its handle. That is, one would find this type of bowl under G 000 v. The subdivision numbers are easily memorized, and it becomes possible to assign a number to a new type and fit it into its place in the corpus. This number deals with form only.

In publishing the corpus, the material will be arranged chronologically with the various forms found in each period grouped according to their form number. Under each form will be a complete description of its ware, decoration, use, and manufacture, with the extent of its geographical distribution throughout Palestine. There will be a series of indexes which will link up references to forms, wares, decoration, etc. Every type will be illustrated in outline, and selected examples by halftone and color plates.

www.ingramcontent.com/pod-product-compliance
Lightning Source LLC
Chambersburg PA
CBHW070516090426
42735CB00012B/2800